Through His Spirit

Through His Spirit

THE PERSON AND UNIQUE
WORK OF THE HOLY SPIRIT

J. VERNON MCGEE

THOMAS NELSON PUBLISHERS®
Nashville

A Division of Thomas Nelson, Inc.
www.ThomasNelson.com

Published in Nashville, Tennessee, by Thomas Nelson, Inc.

Library of Congress Cataloging-in-Publication Data

McGee, J. Vernon (John Vernon), 1904-1988
    Through His Spirit : the person and unique work of the Holy Spirit / J. Vernon McGee.
       p. cm.
       ISBN 0-7852-6294-6
       1. Holy Spirit--Sermons. 2. Sermons, American--20th century.
I. Title.
    BT122.M36 2003
    231'.3--dc21   2002156578

Printed in the United States of America

1 2 3 4 5 6 QWD 08 07 06 05 04 03

CONTENTS

But God has revealed them to us through His Spirit. For the Spirit searches all things, yes, the deep things of God . . . No one knows the things of God except the Spirit of God. (1 Corinthians 2:10–11 NKJV)

Chapter 1

WHO IS THE HOLY SPIRIT?

At the very beginning and end of the Bible, like a great parenthesis, the Spirit of God is mentioned. The Bible opens with:

> *In the beginning God created the heavens and the earth. The earth was without form, and void; and darkness was on the face of the deep. And the Spirit of God was hovering over the face of the waters. Then God said, "Let there be light"; and there was light.* (Genesis 1:1–3 NKJV)

The word for "hovering" means brooding, like a mother hen broods over her little chicks. He brooded over the face of the waters. The Holy Spirit began a ministry at creation that we find Him performing again and again. It is re-creation!

Later, in the Book of Job, we read: "By His Spirit He

adorned the heavens" (Job 26:13 NKJV). Do you know what it means to "adorn"? It means to decorate. The Spirit of God came in after creation and did a work of re-creation, and isn't that a definition of the new birth? Coming in where there is darkness and chaos and bringing regeneration is, I would say, the most important ministry that the Holy Spirit has had since the fall of man in the Garden of Eden.

The closing parenthesis illustrates another work of the Spirit:

> *And the Spirit and the bride say, "Come!" And let him who hears say, "Come!" And let him who thirsts come. Whoever desires, let him take the water of life freely.* (Revelation 22:17 NKJV)

The Spirit of God must move in the world before there can be salvation at all. He is essential; no person can become a child of God apart from the work of the Spirit of God. A right relationship with Christ determines our salvation, but a right relationship with the Holy Spirit determines our sanctification. We are absolutely dependent upon Him not only for life, but for the development and growth of that life. Actually, the Christian life is the Spirit of God living in the believer. This is very important: we need the Person and the power of the Spirit of God.

In between those great parentheses, He is a very prominent subject. In fact, it would be difficult to read and study the Word of God without paying attention to the subject of the Person and work of the Spirit of God. Because there has been such an abnormal emphasis on certain aspects of the work of the Holy Spirit, I'm convinced that we need to put down certain great foundational truths in answer to the question, "Who is the Holy Spirit?"

The first thing we should note is that the Holy Spirit is a person, and He has personality. That doesn't mean He has a body; just having a physical body doesn't make a person. A personality depends on other things, as we will see.

It is necessary, I think, to preface this topic by saying that during the Dark Ages and the inception and rise of Romanism, a great deal of biblical truth was lost to the church because of neglect and the fact that paganism had intruded into the church. The leaders of the Protestant Reformation recovered a great deal of biblical truth that had been lost during that sterile period of the Dark Ages; for instance, Martin Luther's revelations on justification by faith, which shook all of Europe and rang in a religious revolution. During that time there was also John Calvin's distinction between Law and grace, the reformers' emphasis on the inspiration of the Scriptures, and the importance of the Word of God as a rule of life. All of those truths were recovered. But there was some truth that was not recovered at all. In fact, the subject of eschatology (the doctrine of last things—prophecy) has only recently been recovered and is being developed in our days.

But one of the most prominent subjects that was not recovered in the Reformation at all is the Person and work of the Holy Spirit. So, since the days of the Reformation, there have been several movements that have given prominence to this neglected area of truth. The Wesley movement is one such example. John Wesley emphasized the great truth of regeneration. His favorite verse was, "You must be born again" (John 3:7 NKJV). It is said that when asked why he preached so frequently on that topic, Wesley replied, "The reason that I preach so much on 'You must be born again' is because you must be born again." But because of the lack of careful study in this area, some of these movements have led to excesses and extreme interpretations of Scripture.

But in this study we want to examine Scripture in depth and see what the Word of God has to say on this very important subject. We need to recognize that this is one of the great subjects of the Word of God, and it deserves our thoughtful and prayerful study.

One of the main misunderstandings relative to the Holy Spirit is that He's some sort of an influence, a divine emanation, a pervading force, or just an attribute of God. That is the viewpoint that I'm afraid a great many people in our churches have. Yet, in Scripture, the Holy Spirit is identified and designated as a person.

Turning to the Book of Isaiah, notice this first of all:

Come near to Me, hear this: I have not spoken in secret from the beginning; from the time that it was, I was there. And now the Lord GOD and His Spirit have sent Me. (Isaiah 48:16 NKJV)

Actually, this is a prophecy concerning the Messiah. The Lord Jesus said that God (the Father) and God (the Holy

Spirit) sent Him. You see, He spoke of the Holy Spirit as a person separate from God the Father.

And at the time of our Lord's baptism, we read:

> *When all the people were baptized, it came to pass that Jesus also was baptized; and while He prayed, the heaven was opened. And the Holy Spirit descended in bodily form like a dove upon Him, and a voice came from heaven which said, "You are My beloved Son; in You I am well pleased."* (Luke 3:21–22 NKJV)

Again, He is treated as a person.

The Lord Jesus walked on this earth in bodily form, but before He left this world He promised to send another individual (person):

> *And I will pray the Father, and He will give you another Helper . . . the Spirit of truth.* (John 14:16–17 NKJV)

Let's examine one more like this:

> *And do not grieve the Holy Spirit of God, by whom you were sealed for the day of redemption.* (Ephesians 4:30 NKJV)

You cannot grieve a *thing;* you grieve a *person.* The Holy Spirit is a person, and He is grieved by sin in our lives. But we'll look at that more closely later.

The Holy Spirit performs such actions as only a person

could perform, and as a person He has the attributes of a person. For instance, He has a will.

> *But one and the same Spirit works all these things, distributing to each one individually as He wills.* (1 Corinthians 12:11 NKJV)

The Holy Spirit has a will, and only a person has a will.

And like a person, the Holy Spirit also has thoughts and knowledge. Paul wrote to the Romans:

> *Now He who searches the hearts knows what the mind of the Spirit is, because He makes intercession for the saints according to the will of God.* (Romans 8:27 NKJV)

More evidence of His knowledge is found in 1 Corinthians:

> *But God has revealed them to us through His Spirit. For the Spirit searches all things, yes, the deep things of God. For what man knows the things of a man except the spirit of the man which is in him? Even so no one knows the things of God except the Spirit of God.* (1 Corinthians 2:10–11 NKJV)

And I'm sure we would all agree that only a person could love, and the Spirit of God does indeed love. Romans 15:30 (NKJV) refers to "the love of the Spirit," and we know that love is the fruit of the Spirit.

The Holy Spirit can also be treated as a person. For

instance, He can be lied to. You may remember the incident with Ananias and Sapphira and how Peter accused them of lying to the Holy Spirit (see Acts 5:1–11). At another time, he said to the apostles and elders who were arguing, "Why do you test God?" (Acts 15:10 NKJV). In other words, the Holy Spirit can be lied to, and He can be tested.

He can also be resisted. When Stephen stood before the Sanhedrin, he said to those religious rulers:

> *You stiff-necked and uncircumcised in heart and ears! You always resist the Holy Spirit; as your fathers did, so do you.* (Acts 7:51 NKJV)

We've already seen that the Spirit of God can be grieved, but notice what Isaiah said about that great truth of the Old Testament:

> *But they rebelled and grieved His Holy Spirit; so He turned Himself against them as an enemy, and He fought against them.* (Isaiah 63:10 NKJV)

Not only is He grieved, but He can actually be insulted, as the writer to the Hebrews revealed:

> *Of how much worse punishment, do you suppose, will he be thought worthy who has . . . insulted the Spirit of grace?* (Hebrews 10:29 NKJV)

Let's look next at something else that reveals the Holy

Spirit's personality; I'm very eager for you to see this. In the Upper Room Discourse, our Lord said:

> *And I will pray the Father, and He will give you another Helper, that He may abide with you forever . . . But because I have said these things to you, sorrow has filled your heart. Nevertheless I tell you the truth. It is to your advantage that I go away; for if I do not go away, the Helper will not come to you; but if I depart, I will send Him to you.* (John 14:16; 16:6–7 NKJV)

The interesting thing to note here is the pronouns that are used. The word "spirit" is neuter in the Greek. But when He's spoken of as the Holy Spirit, the masculine pronoun is always used. In other words, He's referred to as an individual person. It's tragic that, in some places in Scripture, the pronoun used for the Holy Spirit has been translated as "which" or "that" or "it." It ought not to be that at all! It ought to be "He," because the Greek indicates that it is a masculine pronoun. That is very important!

Now, I hope that somehow I've been able to establish the fact that the Holy Spirit is a person just as the Lord Jesus Christ is a person and God the Father is a person. But that brings me to consider this: the deity of the Holy Spirit.

The Holy Spirit is God. This is very meaningful for us, yet a great many Christians today need to have this truth brought to them. Frankly, most of us feel very much alone and weak today. Maybe we don't even want to call ourselves "saints" because we don't feel like saints, we don't look like saints, and maybe we don't even act like saints. But if you are a child of God, you are indwelt by the Spirit of God and, therefore, have God with you.

> *Do you not know that you are the temple of God and that the Spirit of God dwells in you?* (1 Corinthians 3:16 NKJV)

Athanasius, one of the great saints from the early church, was known to have said, "Wretch, know ye not that you are carrying God with you?" That's what every child of God is doing: you are carrying God with you. So the great truth of this age is that you are not alone! God is not dead; God the Holy Spirit is in the world today, working in the lives and hearts of all who will open their hearts and lives to Him. Now, that's important!

As deity, the Holy Spirit is the third person of the Godhead. We will look at this more closely in the next chapter, but I do want to draw out a few passages to illustrate this.

> *Go therefore and make disciples of all the nations, baptizing them in the name of the Father and of the Son and of the Holy Spirit.* (Matthew 28:19 NKJV)

Baptism is to be in the name of God the Father (the first Person of the Godhead), the Lord Jesus Christ (the second Person of the Godhead), and the Holy Spirit (the third Person of the Godhead). So the Holy Spirit is equal with God.

As we saw a while ago, that principle is illustrated clearly in the Book of Acts:

But Peter said, "Ananias, why has Satan filled your heart to lie to the Holy Spirit and keep back part of the price of the land for yourself? While it remained, was it not your own? And after it was sold, was it not in your own control? Why have you conceived this thing in your heart? You have not lied to men but to God." (Acts 5:3–4 NKJV)

Peter made the Holy Spirit and God synonymous. They didn't lie to just the Holy Spirit, but to God Himself, because the Holy Spirit is God, you see. The Word of God makes that very clear.

Without doubt, one of the most beautiful pictures that we have of the Holy Spirit is displayed in Moses' experience with the children of Israel while they were in the wilderness:

Therefore the people contended with Moses, and said, "Give us water, that we may drink." So Moses said to them, "Why do you contend with me? Why do you tempt the LORD?" And the people thirsted there for water, and the people complained against Moses, and said, "Why is it you have brought us up out of Egypt, to kill us and our children and our livestock with thirst?" So Moses cried out to the LORD, saying, "What shall I do with this people? They are almost ready to stone me!" And the LORD said to Moses, "Go on before the people, and take with you some of the elders of Israel. And take in your hand your rod with which you struck the river, and go. Behold, I will stand before you there on the rock in Horeb; and you shall strike the rock, and water will come out of it, that the people may drink." And Moses did so in the sight of the elders of Israel. So he called the name of the place Massah and Meribah, because of the contention of the children of Israel, and because they tempted the LORD, saying, "Is the LORD among us or not?" (Exodus 17:2–7 NKJV)

Do you see the picture that is there? Moses struck the rock, but who is the rock? The Rock is Christ. Paul said to the Corinthians, "They drank of that spiritual Rock that followed them, and that Rock was Christ" (1 Corinthians 10:4 NKJV). You can fall on the Rock Christ Jesus for salvation, but no human effort is able to get water from this Rock. Only when the Rock was struck did it bring forth life-giving waters. Jesus was crucified, and nothing short of believing that He died in your place and bore your sins on that cross will save you. The smitten rock is a picture of the death of Jesus Christ.

And what of the water? The water is one of the finest figures we have of the Holy Spirit of God. You don't have a prettier picture than that. Moses struck the rock and water flowed forth. God gave His Son to die upon the cross, and then the Son sent the Holy Spirit—the water flowed forth into the world.

There's another picture of the Holy Spirit recorded in the wonderful dedication chapter of Isaiah, which set him aside for the service of God:

Also I heard the voice of the Lord, saying: "Whom shall I send, and who will go for Us?" Then I said, "Here am I! Send me." And He said, "Go, and tell this people:

> *'Keep on hearing, but do not understand; keep on seeing,
> but do not perceive.' Make the heart of this people dull,
> and their ears heavy, and shut their eyes; lest they see
> with their eyes, and hear with their ears, and under-
> stand with their heart, and return and be healed."*
> (Isaiah 6:8–10 NKJV)

What did Isaiah say? "I heard the voice of the Lord." But in
the Book of Acts, Paul the apostle referred to this particular
passage of Scripture, saying:

> *So when they did not agree among themselves, they
> departed after Paul had said one word: "The Holy Spirit
> spoke rightly through Isaiah the prophet to our fathers."*
> (Acts 28:25 NKJV)

Paul said it was the Holy Spirit who spoke to Isaiah, so we
have here a clear reference to the fact that the Holy Spirit *is*
God, my beloved.

The Holy Spirit has all the attributes of deity: omniscience, omnipresence, omnipotence. Omniscience means
He has all knowledge, as God does. Paul said that the
Spirit of God is our teacher today and the only One who
can take the Word of God and make it real to us. Because
"'eye has not seen, nor ear heard, nor have entered into the
heart of man the things which God has prepared for those
who love Him.' But God has revealed them to us through
His Spirit" (1 Corinthians 2:9–10 NKJV). Only the Spirit
of God knows the mind of God because He *is* God, you

see. The Spirit alone can take the things of God and make them real to us; He alone can make us understand.

I'm not disturbed when unbelievers say they don't believe in the virgin birth. Of course they don't. In fact, I hope they don't! Anytime an unsaved man says, "I believe in the virgin birth," he upsets me terribly because he is contradicting the Bible. The Bible says you can't know it, my friends, until the Spirit of God makes it real to you. We need to emphasize today that only the Spirit of God can open this Book, and that's one of the reasons why it's not an interesting book to a great many people. You can get facts, but you can't get truth until the Spirit of God is your teacher.

The Holy Spirit is also omnipresent. That means He is everywhere at the same time. But that's not all. It means *all* of Him is everywhere at the same time. You may ask me to explain that, but I can't. I don't understand it, but that's what the Word of God teaches. He's the infinite God, and all of Him is everywhere at the same time.

David was so amazed with this. He wrote:

> *Where can I go from Your Spirit? Or where can I flee from Your presence? If I ascend into heaven, You are there; if I make my bed in hell* [the grave], *behold, You are there. If I take the wings of the morning, and dwell in the uttermost parts of the sea, even there Your hand shall lead me, and Your right hand shall hold me.* (Psalm 139:7–10 NKJV)

The Spirit of God is everywhere. He's omnipresent, for He is God.

There are many symbols of the Holy Spirit, and I'm confident God gave them to us to help us to understand who He is. In closing, I want to mention just one symbol, and that is the dove. I believe it is one of the loveliest pictures given of Him. Turning again to the account of Jesus' baptism, we read:

> *And the Holy Spirit descended in bodily form like a dove upon Him, and a voice came from heaven which said, "You are My beloved Son; in You I am well pleased."* (Luke 3:22 NKJV)

By the way, there we have the Trinity again: God the Father speaking from heaven, God the Son being baptized, and the Spirit of God coming upon Him like a dove. John made reference to this incident in his Gospel:

> *"This is He of whom I said, 'After me comes a Man who is preferred before me, for He was before me.' I did not know Him; but that He should be revealed to Israel, therefore I came baptizing with water." And John bore witness, saying, "I saw the Spirit descending from heaven like a dove, He remained upon Him. I did not know Him, but He who sent me to baptize with water said to me, 'Upon whom you see the Spirit descending, and remaining on Him, this is He who baptizes with the Holy Spirit.'"* (John 1:30–33 NKJV)

The dove image also appears in the story of Noah, who sent out of the ark a raven and a dove. The raven did not come back. He found a dead carcass that he could make a meal of, and it was for him a wonderful thing. But not the dove. The dove flew over the flooded area and the land marred by judgment, and he could find rest only in the ark.

The dove speaks of the Holy Spirit, and thus the Holy Spirit is today in the world. Like that dove, I don't think the Spirit of God is happy in the world. But He's here on heavenly business, and that's to call the church out of the world. When that's completed, He'll take the church and present it to the Father.

You and I are living in a world in which the Spirit of God has been almost crowded out, even by believers. We must recognize that we need the Spirit of God to bring the reality of Christ into our lives. We have hungry hearts, but we will never be satisfied with material things. Some of the most unhappy people are those who have everything that this world offers. What we really need is a fresh infilling of the Spirit of God in our lives.

The Spirit of God must be in the hearts and lives of believers today if we are going to see any movement of God at all, my beloved. That's His method, and that's His way. Materialism and criticism and philosophy have crowded Him out, yet they bring no happiness into this world. How we need God on the scene, and only the Spirit of God can make the Lord Jesus real today! That's the reason why we want to study the Person and the work of the Holy Spirit of God.

Chapter 2

HOW CAN GOD EXIST
IN THREE PERSONS?

The great English poet Samuel Taylor Coleridge, in a conversation with Robert Browning, remarked, "I read all your poetry, but nine-tenths of it I do not understand." Robert Browning answered him by saying, "Sir, a person of your caliber ought to be satisfied if he understands one-tenth." Well, I have spent more than a quarter of a century in serious study of the Word of God, and I confess to my appalling ignorance in certain areas, especially in the subject of the Trinity. If you could have met me the year I graduated from seminary, you would have heard me give absolute answers to all of your questions. But I am unable to do that today. In fact, I would be content if I understood one-tenth of the great truth concerning our triune God.

I assure you that with all my heart I believe in the Trinity. I revel and rejoice in it, believing that it is not only a great truth but also one of the unique truths of the Christian faith. But I confess that I find it to be an enigmatic mystery, an inscrutable riddle. I find that it is complicated, complex, bewildering, and impossible to explain. Why?

One reason is that the Trinity is not geared to this mechanical age. Tensions and pressures hurry us through life. A cartoonist has pictured a man sitting in a one-counter restaurant, giving his order to the waitress. He is saying, "I have to be at work in twenty-three minutes. I want one-minute oatmeal, three-minute eggs, two-minute bacon, forty-five-second toast, and instant coffee." An age that goes at a pace like that is not an age that will know very much about the Trinity, for the Trinity cannot be explained in just a few moments. It is doubtful if it can ever be satisfactorily explained, yet we need to study it carefully.

For several hundred years after the apostles lived, the Trinity was a most important subject to intelligent men. Men like Irenaeus, Tertullian, Athanasius, Origen, and Augustine gave themselves to the study of this great doctrine. It was the all-engrossing topic that men of keen intellect spent their time pondering. As a result, the doctrine of the Trinity broadly affected European life for centuries. From the day of the apostles until about the seventh century, it was very important to multitudes of people. The economic, political, and social spheres were all essentially influenced by this truth. Rulers reigned, armies marched, and diplomats convened as this truth helped shape the destiny of Europe.

All so-called theological liberalism is basically off at this point. Behind the denial of the deity of Christ is the denial of the Trinity. This denial came into America by way of New England through the Congregational churches, which eventually became largely Unitarian churches. There is an ancient adage that warns that those who try to understand the Trinity lose their minds and those who deny the Trinity lose their souls. We are caught in that kind of dilemma. Although we will not be able to understand it fully, or perhaps not even satisfactorily, we will at least stand on the fringe of this great truth and worship.

We will look at the *definition* of the Trinity, then the *declaration* in Scripture of the Trinity, and finally *illustrations* of the Trinity from nature.

THE TRINITY DEFINED

First is the definition of the Trinity. What do we mean by "the Trinity"? We mean three Persons in the Godhead. There are two extremes that we need to avoid. They are like Scylla on one hand and Charybdis on the other (two equally dangerous monsters), and we need to sail our little bark between them. The initial danger, when speaking of the Trinity, is to have in mind three gods. That is a false concept. Then there is the other extreme of holding that the one God has expressed Himself in three different ways, which is also false. This error, known as modal-trinitarianism, was thoroughly answered by some of the giants of the faith whom we have already named.

I turn now to what I believe is the best statement made

on this subject. It is in the Westminster Confession of Faith. The question is asked: "How many Persons are there in the Godhead?" The answer is: "There are three Persons in the Godhead: the Father, the Son, and the Holy Ghost; and these three are one God, the same in substance, equal in power and glory." That definition is the finest to be found.

Now notice that three persons constitute one God. Peter, James, and John are not a trinity. They are three persons, but they are not the same, they are not equal. There are three chairs before me. They look alike and probably are constructed of the same material—possibly of the same tree—yet they are not a trinity.

God is one Being, and yet He is three Persons. However, these three have one nature. For instance, some like to make a distinction by saying that God is holy, Christ is love, and the Holy Spirit is infinite. Such is a false distinction, for God is holy, Christ is holy, and the Holy Spirit is holy; God is love (that is one of His definitions), Christ is love, and the Holy Spirit is love; God is infinite, Christ is infinite, and the Holy Spirit is infinite.

The three Persons are also the same in their attributes, in their will, and in their purpose. What one wills, all will. When the Lord Jesus came to earth, He made this very clear: "I have come to do My Father's will" (see John 14 and 15). What He had come to do was in harmony with the Father, for all three were in agreement. He came to do the Father's will; He came to do His own will, which was evident; and He came to do the will of the Holy Spirit—He was led and guided by the Spirit of God.

Each one is God. Christ did not become a Son over time. He was always the only begotten Son of God. You see, God is called the "Everlasting Father" (Isaiah 9:6 NKJV), and you cannot have an everlasting Father unless you have an everlasting Son. There never was a time when Christ *became* the Son—He eternally occupies that position in the Trinity.

Another false way of stating it is to say that God is the Father, Christ is the Son, and the Holy Spirit is sort of like the Grandson. There was never a time when God was not the Father, there was never a time when Christ was not the Son, and there was never a time when the Holy Spirit was not the Holy Spirit. There are some who will say that because the Lord Jesus Christ came to this earth as a man, He is not equal with the Father. This is also wrong, for He said, "I and My Father are one" (John 10:30 NKJV).

They have the same nature. There are not three gods and they are never opposed to one another. What one does, all of them do. The clarity of this fact can do nothing but make us stand on the fringe and know that we are in the presence of the Infinite.

The Trinity Declared by Scripture

We come now to the declaration in Scripture of the Trinity. I hasten to say that the word "trinity" is not used in Scripture. But neither is the word "atonement" used in the New Testament (the word incorrectly translated as "atonement" in Romans 5:11 (KJV) is actually "reconciliation"). But although the word does not appear in the New Testament, it certainly teaches what the Old Testament presents as the Atonement. It is not necessary to have the word, because that which the word signifies is taught in the New Testament Scripture. Since the word "trinity" does not appear in Scripture, does the Bible actually teach the doctrine of the Trinity? If it does not, we can dismiss the subject and forget about it. But if the Word of God does teach the Trinity, then we should believe it.

Someone may say, "Before I believe it, I want to understand it." If truth is only that which we understand, may I say that there is not much that is true today, for we are quite limited in our understanding. On such a basis, trigonometry and organic chemistry are not true because I don't understand them. In college, I had no desire to understand them, and today I still have no desire to understand these two subjects. Yet I do not take the awkward and ignorant position that they are not true subjects—they are. Thankfully, truth is not limited to my little mind or to your little mind. There are those today who, because they cannot understand the Trinity, want to dismiss it. However, the real question is: does the Word of God teach the Trinity?

The Trinity in the Old Testament

The Old Testament clearly teaches the Trinity. The verse of Scripture that is probably the greatest doctrinal statement in the Old Testament is found in the Book of Deuteronomy:

> *Hear, O Israel: The LORD our God, the LORD is one!*
> (Deuteronomy 6:4 NKJV)

If you want a literal translation, it is, "Hear, O Israel: the LORD our plural God is one God!" The word translated "one" is *echad*, the same word used back in Genesis 2:24 (NKJV) when God said, concerning Adam and Eve, "And they shall become one flesh." Two persons become one. In that mysterious relationship of marriage, two people are made one, which is evident always in the child. They shall be one flesh, though two—two in one. This is the word used in Deuteronomy 6:4 (my paraphrase), "Hear, O Israel: *Elohim*—our plural God, our Trinity, tripersonality—is one God!" The mysterious One, like Adam and Eve made one flesh, is three Persons in one. That is a wonderful truth and unfathomable by human reason.

The Old Testament repeatedly declares the plurality of God. If you go back to the first chapter of Genesis, you will see this again:

> *Then God said, "Let Us make man in Our image, according to Our likeness; let them have dominion over the fish of the sea, over the birds of the air, and over the cattle, over all the earth and over every creeping thing that creeps on the earth." So God created man in His own image; in the image of God He created him; male and female He created them.* (Genesis 1:26–27 NKJV)

Notice that God said, "Let *Us* make man in *Our* image." It is plural.

Then in the eleventh chapter of Genesis, at the Tower of Babel, God said:

> *"Come, let Us go down and there confuse their language, that they may not understand one another's speech." So the LORD scattered them abroad from there over the face of all the earth, and they ceased building the city.* (Genesis 11:7–8 NKJV)

We see here that the Lord scattered them, but He said, "Let *Us* go down." The Trinity came down, but He is still one God.

Moving on in the Old Testament, we find that Isaiah said:

> *Also I heard the voice of the Lord, saying: "Whom shall I send, and who will go for Us?" Then I said, "Here am I! Send me."* (Isaiah 6:8 NKJV)

Before this, Isaiah had gone into the temple and heard the seraphim saying, "Holy, holy, holy" (Isaiah 6:3 NKJV)—they said "holy" not twice, not four times, but three times. It was a praise to the triune God. Holy is the Father, holy is the Son, and holy is the Spirit.

In Ecclesiastes, we read the familiar words, "Remember now your Creator in the days of your youth" (12:1 NKJV). The word translated "Creator" is *Boreacho,* which means "Creators," plural. "Remember now thy Creators, thy Trinity"—for the Trinity is involved in creation, as you well know. We are told that God the Father was the Creator, "In the beginning God created . . ." Both the Gospel of John (1:3) and the Epistle to the Colossians (1:16) tell us that the Lord Jesus Christ was the Creator. Also, we are told that the

Holy Spirit of God was the Creator: "The Spirit of God was hovering over the face of the waters" (Genesis 1:2 NKJV). Thus it is evident that the Trinity was involved in creation just as the Trinity is involved in redemption.

In the Old Testament, Israel witnessed to a polytheistic world—a civilization with many gods—concerning the unity of the Godhead. That was the mission of Israel in the ancient world. The mission of the church in this day is to a world not given to polytheism (the worship of many gods), but to atheism (the worship of no god). To our godless civilization, we are to witness to the Trinity. For that reason, the Unitarian doctrine that God exists only in one person is a damnable heresy that has injured America more than any other thing. It is what has softened and weakened this great country of ours.

The Trinity in the New Testament

The record in the Gospels of the baptism of the Lord Jesus Christ graphically presents the Trinity. At the time the Lord Jesus was baptized, He saw the Holy Spirit as a dove coming upon Him, and the voice of the Father from heaven spoke saying, "This is My beloved Son, in whom I am well pleased" (Matthew 3:17 NKJV). The Trinity—the Father, Son, and Holy Spirit—is clearly brought before us on this occasion.

Again, in the baptismal formula that Jesus gave to His apostles when He sent them out, He said, "Baptiz[e] them in the name of the Father and of the Son and of the Holy Spirit" (Matthew 28:19 NKJV).

Paul, in his apostolic benediction, included the three Persons of the Godhead:

The grace of the **Lord Jesus Christ**, *and the love of* **God**, *and the communion of the* **Holy Spirit** *be with you all. Amen.* (2 Corinthians 13:14 NKJV, emphasis mine)

The Lord Jesus even taught His disciples the doctrine of the Trinity:

And I will pray the **Father,** *and He will give you another* **Helper** [like I am, on the same par with Me], *that He may abide with you forever.* (John 14:16 NKJV, emphasis mine)

The New Testament abounds with the teaching of the Trinity, for it repeatedly names the three Persons of the Godhead. We have a *Father* who is God:

To all who are in Rome, beloved of God, called to be saints: Grace to you and peace from **God** *our* **Father** *and the Lord Jesus Christ.* (Romans 1:7 NKJV, emphasis mine)

We have presented to us in the New Testament a *Son* who is God.

But to the **Son** *He says: "Your throne, O God, is forever and ever; a scepter of righteousness is the scepter of Your kingdom."* (Hebrews 1:8 NKJV, emphasis mine)

Also the *Holy Spirit* is presented as God. At the incident involving Ananias and Sapphira, as I've mentioned, Peter said:

> *Ananias, why has Satan filled your heart to lie to the* **Holy Spirit** *and keep back part of the price of the land for yourself? While it remained, was it not your own? And after it was sold, was it not in your own control? Why have you conceived this thing in your heart? You have not lied to men but to* **God**. (Acts 5:3–4 NKJV, emphasis mine)

Peter was saying, "You have lied to the Holy Spirit, and when you have lied to the Holy Spirit you have lied to God." Why? Because the Holy Spirit is God.

THE TRINITY ILLUSTRATED BY NATURE

I repeat the question: is it possible to understand the Trinity? If the answer must be either yes or no, it has to be an emphatic *no*. The centuries have revealed that the intellect of the genius, the perspicuity of the philosopher, the comprehension of the scientist, and the lucidity of the orator have not been enough to make clear the Trinity. The reason is this: there are no perfect examples that can be used, because it is impossible to demonstrate the infinite God by finite creation. We cannot employ the creation to illustrate adequately the Creator in His Person.

Now it is true that the *love* of God can be illustrated by human love. You can take that feeling of love and translate it into human terminology. You see a mother bending over the crib of her little baby and somehow it illustrates something of God's great pulsating love for us. But in nature you find no such illustration for the Trinity. Yet I shall dare to pull in several illustrations from nature that may be somewhat helpful.

Man

First of all, I want to look at man himself.

> *Now may the God of peace Himself sanctify you completely* [your total personality]*; and may your whole spirit, soul, and body be preserved blameless at the coming of our Lord Jesus Christ.* (1 Thessalonians 5:23 NKJV)

Man was created in the image of God, and so man is a trinity—body, soul, and spirit.

Believe me, if we could understand human nature, we would have a better understanding of God. But we do not understand even ourselves. Psychology has wrestled with this. When psychology began, it dealt with only the spirit or the soul. Then it found it was on the wrong track, so it swung over to the opposite extreme, as in my day when the psychology studied in college was behaviorism. It taught that we are only physical, like a series of push buttons. You push *this* button and you get *that* reaction. The difficulty is that you push a certain button on one fellow and get a certain reaction, but you push the same button on another fellow and you get a different reaction.

Since that theory did not work, psychology changed its mind again and said that we are more than body and more than just spirit. Psychology now admits that man is a threefold being: man is sarcous, man is psychic, and man is pneumatic. In other words, there is the body, there is the psychological part, and there is the spiritual part. We are more than body; we are more than just mind; we are more than spirit.

By the way, I am thankful that we are more than spirit. What a relief it was to me when I found out that I was not going to be an angel. When I was a little fellow in Sunday school, they taught us to sing, "I want to be an angel, and with the angels sing." Well, *I* never wanted to be an angel because I thought angels flitted around without bodies, which never suited me at all. I am thankful that throughout eternity we are to have bodies. We have been created a trinity—body, soul, and spirit.

When we say that we do not understand the Trinity, we must confess that neither do we understand ourselves. When we better understand man, we shall understand something of the Trinity that is God.

Music

Let me move now into another realm of nature—the field of music. I am told that in music there are seven tones on the major scale but that there are only three structural tones. These are the principal chords: the tonic, the subdominant, and the dominant. These are the three major tones, and out of them comes all of our music. You cannot have harmony without these three.

There is the harmony of heaven. The Word of God speaks of it before man was created: "when the morning stars sang together, and all the sons of God shouted for joy" (Job 38:7 NKJV). This heavenly music was based on a trinity—you cannot have harmony without it. Thus in the realm of music you have the three that make one, and the one is harmony.

Water

Let us move further into nature and consider water. Water is used in the Scriptures as a picture of God—He is spoken of as water. Listen to the psalm that is David's heart cry:

> *As the deer pants for the water brooks, so pants my soul for You, O God. My soul thirsts for God, for the living God.* (Psalm 42:1–2 NKJV)

David was saying, "What the water brook is to a little animal, that is what God is to me."

Then notice another psalm in which water repeatedly pictures God:

> *You visit the earth and water it, You greatly enrich it; the river of God is full of water; You provide their grain, for so You have prepared it.* (Psalm 65:9 NKJV)

Throughout the Old Testament water is a picture of God, so that when we come to the New Testament it is not surprising to hear the Lord Jesus cry on that last day of the feast, "If anyone thirsts, let him come to Me and drink" (John 7:37 NKJV).

Water is also a picture of the Trinity, for water exists in three forms, in three states. It exists in flowing water, it exists in ice, and it exists in steam. They are the same substance, but they are absolutely three different things. Ice, I would suggest, reminds us of God the Father—stability, immutability. Steam reminds us of the Holy Spirit—the power of God. Water reminds us of the Lord Jesus Christ— the Water of Life today.

Light

For our final illustration, let us consider light. We are told that God *dwells* in light and that He *is* light. "In Him is no darkness at all" (1 John 1:5 NKJV). One of the glorious prospects of our future eternal home is that there will be no night there.

Light is probably the most expressive and adequate illustration that we have of the Trinity. God is light; God is holy. It is the attribute of the Father, but of Christ also. He declared this attribute when a great sinner was brought to Him: "I am the light of the world" (John 8:12 NKJV). He was manifest. He is the "light" in John 1:5 (NKJV): "And the light shines in the darkness, and the darkness did not comprehend it."

The Holy Spirit is called light. He was pictured in the lampstand in the tabernacle, and then later the temple bore lights that spoke of the Holy Spirit of God. Zechariah was given a vision of the lampstand, which was supplied with oil directly from the olive trees instead of through a middle-man. In case there was any question, God provided the explanation: "'Not by might nor by power, but by My *Spirit*,' says the LORD of hosts" (Zechariah 4:6 NKJV, emphasis mine).

In the Book of Revelation, John was given the vision of God's throne, which is characterized by light:

> *And from the throne proceeded lightnings, thunderings, and voices. Seven lamps of fire were burning before the throne, which are the seven Spirits of God* [the complete Spirit of God—the Holy Spirit]. (Revelation 4:5 NKJV)

Light is probably the best picture we have of God. Paul brought all three Persons together under this figure:

> *For it is the God who commanded light to shine out of darkness, who has shone in our hearts to give the light of the knowledge of the glory of God in the face of Jesus Christ.* (2 Corinthians 4:6 NKJV)

Notice that we have been called out of darkness into His marvelous light. We today are to walk in light. We have made the error of talking about *how* we walk rather than *where* we walk. When a man walks according to the *how*, he always pleases himself, because he can make up his own little rules and say he is spiritual. It is not *how* we walk but *where* we walk that is all-important. Are we walking in the light of the Word of God?

Every ray of light is pure white, and we always associate that white with God. You can pass a ray of light through a prism, which will divide it into three primary colors. These three elementary colors are yellow, red, and blue. Yellow speaks of the holiness of the Father; red speaks of God the Son who shed His blood for you and for me; blue speaks of the Holy Spirit, for blue is the color of truth, and He is the Spirit of truth. You can push the yellow, red, and blue lights back through the prism and get one white light—three in one.

I am told that the flowers we see do not have any color whatsoever, that actually they and everything else are colorless. I look at these multicolored flowers and am told that although they are colorless, they have the power to absorb or reject the light rays falling upon them. For example, the yellow daffodil absorbs all the color rays except yellow, and since it rejects yellow, I see it as a yellow daffodil! I don't understand that at all. And if I cannot understand light, do you expect me to understand the Trinity? Yet this illustration from nature helps me.

The Trinity's Plan for Man

Back in the beginning (when I say "beginning," I mean before God had created anything), there was no vast universe as we have it today, there were no angels, there was no creation at all. God was alone. Now consider this: God was love, yet you cannot have love unless you have an object of love. But there has always been the Trinity and the love they have for themselves. God the Father loves the Son, He is careful to tell us that. The Son loves the Father, He tells us so. The Holy Spirit loves both of them, and because of His love for them He is in the world today—this sin-stained world—carrying out their work and His work.

Back in eternity when God was alone, this great plan by which He is working today opened up for Him as the best plan. We know now that it meant He was to have a creature called man and that this little man would lift his fist in rebellion against his holy God. And his holy God must strike him down. A holy God would be just and righteous to breathe this little world out of existence. And, friends, He would not miss it, for He has other universes bigger and, I think, better than this. Why does He hang on to it? Because in His plan, He wants fellowship with that man down there in sin.

Perhaps at that time the Father said, "I will have to judge that man." The Son said, "Because We love him, I'll go down and die for him." The Father said, "I'll send You." And the Holy Spirit said, "I'll go down afterward, and though I am blasphemed against and insulted, I shall stay in the world with that little miserable man and try to bring him back into a relationship with Us."

This is the reason the Scripture says that Christ was the Lamb slain from the foundation of the world. Friends, the Cross was not an ambulance that God sent to the scene of an accident. The Cross is not God's emergency air-raid shelter that He put up hurriedly to meet a surprise attack. Redemption was in God's great plan at the beginning. According to Galatians 4:4, the Father sent the Son to earth in the fullness of time, and

He came forth—born of a woman, made under the law—that He might redeem those who were under the law and that He might redeem you today.

The triune God is involved not only in creation but in your redemption and in my redemption. God the Father loves you; He sent His Son. God the Son loves you; He died for you. And God the Holy Spirit loves you, for He is now at your heart's door knocking, wanting to come into your life.

Our triune God! No, you will not understand Him. He would not be God if you could. But you can bow in adoration and praise and yield that little, stubborn, rebellious heart to Him.

Chapter 3

THE HOLY SPIRIT AND
THE WORD OF GOD

What is the relationship of the Holy Spirit to the Word of God? The best place to turn for an answer to that question is the Scriptures—what does the Word of God have to say?

In his second epistle, Peter told of his experience on the Mount of Transfiguration:

For we did not follow cunningly devised fables when we made known to you the power and coming of our Lord Jesus Christ, but were eyewitnesses of His majesty. For He received from God the Father honor and glory when such a voice came to Him from the Excellent Glory: "This is My beloved Son, in whom I am well pleased." And we heard this voice which came from heaven when we were with Him on the holy mountain. And so we have the prophetic word confirmed, which you do well to heed as a light that shines in a dark place, until the day dawns and the morning star rises in your hearts. (2 Peter 1:16–19 NKJV)

Peter was an eyewitness, yet what he was saying here is that it is better to have the Word of God than to have been an eyewitness. A great many people think, "Oh, if only I could have been with Peter. If only I could have seen those things." Friend, you have something even better. You have the Word of God. It will speak directly to you if you will open your heart and allow it to speak.

The Word of God is better than seeing and hearing. It is a light, a lamp, a source of light like the sun in the sky. It is a centrifugal force. As the sun gives out its light, throwing it out to the universe, so the Word of God sends out a light, a force, and a power. The Word of God is the only physical miracle that we have from God in this hour in which we live.

Knowing this first, that no prophecy of Scripture is of any private interpretation. (2 Peter 1:20)

Simon Peter said that this is the first thing we are to know. The word "knowing" is a knowledge that comes not only from facts that can be ascertained—if you have an honest heart, you can find out whether the facts in the Bible are accurate or not—but these are things that you can know by the Holy Spirit making them real to you. I have long since passed the stage when I wanted the Bible proved to me. When I was in college, I did want the Bible proved to me; if I found that archaeology had dug up a spadeful of dirt somewhere that proved a fact in the Bible, I would clap my hands like a little child and shout, "Wonderful!" I don't do that anymore. I don't need a spadeful of turned-up dirt to prove to me that the Bible is true. The Spirit of God Himself has made the Word of God real to my heart, and I know there is a transforming power in it. This is something that we can *know*, and the facts, confirmed by the Holy Spirit, make it real to us.

> *For prophecy never came by the will of man, but holy men of God spoke as they were moved* [or as they were carried along] *by the Holy Spirit.* (2 Peter 1:21 NKJV)

"Holy men" does not mean that the writers were some super-duper saints. It means holy in the sense of being set apart for this particular office. If you are a holy Christian, it means that you are set apart for Jesus Christ.

"As they were moved by the Holy Spirit" is a delightful figure of speech. The Greek actually portrays the idea of a sailing vessel. The wind gets into those great sails, bellies them out, and moves the ship along. That is the way the Holy Spirit moved these men. It is wonderful to see how God could take each man and use him, without changing his style or interfering with his personality, to write His Word so that His message came across. While Paul the apostle wrote eloquent Greek, Peter the apostle—since he was a fisherman and Greek was his second language—wrote Greek that was not quite as good. Yet God used both of these men to write exactly what He wanted to say—so much so that, if

God spoke out of heaven today, He would have to repeat Himself, because He has said all that He has to say to mankind. God has gotten His Word to us through men of different personalities and different skills.

> *Of this salvation the prophets have inquired and searched carefully, who prophesied of the grace that would come to you, searching what, or what manner of time, the Spirit of Christ who was in them was indicating when He testified beforehand the sufferings of Christ and the glories that would follow.* (1 Peter 1:10–11 NKJV)

This tells us specifically that the prophets of the Old Testament wrote by the Spirit of Christ. This is only one of the many statements contained in the Word of God declaring that the Old Testament was inspired of God. These men wrote by the "Spirit of Christ."

David gave us further evidence of the Holy Spirit's inspiration of Scripture:

> *The Spirit of the LORD spoke by me, and His word was on my tongue.* (2 Samuel 23:2 NKJV)

Then, turning to the Book of Acts, notice that Peter confirmed it:

> *Men and brethren, this Scripture had to be fulfilled, which the Holy Spirit spoke before by the mouth of David concerning Judas.* (Acts 1:16 NKJV)

So Scripture makes it very clear that the Spirit of God is the author of the Word of God.

The Bible is the written Word, a human book; it's also a divine book, God's Word. For this reason, I call it a man-book and a God-book. It is very much like the Lord Jesus Christ, who is called the Living Word. He was a man, but He was also God. Likewise, this written Word is also a living Word. Jesus was never any more man because He was God, and He was never any less God because He was man.

The Bible is a God-book, but it's also a perfectly human book because, frankly, it was given in language that man can understand. God wants to communicate with us. For that reason, He chose both princes and paupers to write it. He drew from the most brilliant men and the most ignorant men so that He could speak to everybody. I do not think there have been two men who could surpass Moses and Paul the apostle in intelligence. But I'll be honest with you and say that there are some canonical writers at the other end of the IQ scale. Yet God could use and communicate through them all.

God spoke in His Book in a way that He's not speaking anywhere else today. He doesn't speak through some prophet or miracle worker today. Having given us the intelligence and language to study it, today He speaks to us through a book—a book that we can have confidence is the Word of God. The Bible is a God-book, and that must be taken in consideration when we begin to study it.

There are three kinds of man in the world: the natural man, the carnal man, and the spiritual man. The natural man is unsaved; he's natural, just like the day he came into the world. He is born a sinner, like we all are, but he has not been born again.

> *But the natural man does not receive the things of the Spirit of God, for they are foolishness to him; nor can he know them, because they are spiritually discerned.* (1 Corinthians 2:14 NKJV)

What are "the things of the Spirit of God"? It's the Bible— and that is what makes it different from every other book. Any other book that has been written by a man, can be understood by a man.

When I was a student in college, I had the high-minded notion that anything that a man wrote I could understand. Well, I have found that that isn't true. Certainly I cannot understand the Word of God until the Spirit of God opens my heart and mind to understand. You see, God's Book is closed to the natural man. The natural man cannot receive the things of God. Why not? Because they are foolishness to him. If you are not a Christian, my friend, what I am saying seems foolish to you. If it doesn't, there is something wrong with you or there is something wrong with me—one of us is wrong. God says that the natural man finds the preaching of the cross of Christ for salvation foolish. It simply does not make sense to him.

Carnal believers don't understand, either. Paul wrote to the Corinthians, "And I, brethren, could not speak to you as to spiritual people but as to carnal, as to babes in Christ"

(1 Corinthians 3:1 NKJV). That's where the trouble is in the church today—carnal believers. God can't speak to a great many people who are born again. The reason is because they have no understanding of the Word of God. They do not study the Word of God, and they have no hunger or desire for it whatsoever.

My friend, the Geiger counter for spirituality is your understanding and knowledge of God's Word. And, in that, the Spirit of God must be our teacher. The wonderful part is that He has a way of opening it to the most brilliant mind and also to the simplest mind—that's reason for some of us to rejoice. He can open it to anyone. That's why some rather simple folk understand the Word of God better than some highly intellectual person understands it—they have the Spirit of God teaching and leading them.

The Spirit understands God; we don't. Do you know how God feels or what He thinks? He says, "For as the heavens are higher than the earth, so are My ways higher than your ways, and My thoughts than your thoughts" (Isaiah 55:9 NKJV). You can't know what God is thinking. So the Spirit of God, who gave the book, is now the teacher of it. The Author is here to lead and guide us to all truth. We need to recognize that we are dealing with a book that's different from any other. That being the case, let me give you just a few very simple rules for studying the Word.

First, begin with prayer. Why? Because, my friend, we can't gain this knowledge by eye or ear or cogitation. You'll miss a great deal of the truth that is contained in the Word if you try to go that route. That's been demonstrated down through the history of the world by brilliant men who have been able to understand certain facts about the Bible, but who have never been able to grasp the truth of the Word of God. It's amazing how they have missed it.

Joseph Renan, one of the most intelligent French skeptics, wrote a life of Jesus. The factual part of it is probably the finest that's ever been written. But when you come to his interpretation of Jesus, a six-year-old child could reveal more sense than Renan revealed. What was his problem? The natural man can handle facts, because the Bible is a human book. So as long as Renan stayed on the human side, dealing with facts and history and poetry, he was brilliant. But the minute he moved over to the spiritual interpretation, he fell to pieces.

My beloved, I've said this before, but when an unbeliever says he does not believe the virgin birth or that he doesn't understand the Trinity, I say, "Amen, Hallelujah!" I am very happy for that, and do you know why? Because if a lost man understands spiritual truths, he disproves the Word of God. So when an intelligent but unsaved man says, "That business of the Trinity is simply silly," I thank him, because he has merely confirmed the Word of God.

Only the Spirit of God speaking to your heart, my beloved, can reveal the truths of His Word to you. So every time you take the Word of God out to study it, don't think that by your brilliance you are going to be able to get all of its truth. The Spirit of God will have to be your teacher; He alone can take things of Christ and show them to you.

And the way to begin is with prayer. I think this is a good prayer: "Open my eyes, that I may see wondrous things from Your law" (Psalm 119:18 NKJV). Paul prayed that kind of prayer for the Ephesians:

> *That the God of our Lord Jesus Christ, the Father of glory, may give to you the spirit of wisdom and revelation in the knowledge of Him, the eyes of your understanding being enlightened; that you may know what is the hope of His calling, what are the riches of the glory of His inheritance in the saints, and what is the exceeding greatness of His power toward us who believe, according to the working of His mighty power which He worked in Christ when He raised Him from the dead and seated Him at His right hand in the heavenly places.* (Ephesians 1:17–20 NKJV)

When Paul was ready to pray the greatest prayer for the Ephesians, he didn't pray for their healing, that they would be successful, or that they would be kept from harm and persecution. He prayed that they might be filled with the knowledge of the will of God, and that the Spirit would open the Word of God so they'd understand it. My friend, that's the greatest prayer you can pray for anyone—that they might understand the Word of God and, therefore, the will of God.

An interesting thing to note is that the Spirit of God *wants* to teach us; that's part of His ministry. The Lord Jesus said:

But the Helper, the Holy Spirit, whom the Father will send in My name, He will teach you all things, and bring to your remembrance all things that I said to you. (John 14:26 NKJV)

He is the great Teacher, and He wants to teach us.

When I was in college, how I tried to get under Dr. Townsend, the great Shakespeare scholar. I never shall forget the thrill I had that first day I sat down in his class. But, friends, there's something more wonderful than that—the Holy Spirit of God will teach you the Word of God. Oh, let Him be your teacher today.

However, when He, the Spirit of truth, has come, He will guide you into all truth; for He will not speak on His own authority, but whatever He hears He will speak; and He will tell you things to come. He will glorify Me, for He will take of what is Mine and declare it to you. All things that the Father has are Mine. Therefore I said that He will take of Mine and declare it to you. (John 16:13–14 NKJV)

What a wonderful thing it is that the Spirit of God will take the Word of God and reveal Christ to us in it. Therefore, when we begin to study the Word of God, we need to lift our hearts to the Father in prayer, asking Him to let the Spirit of God lead and guide us.

The second thing that is essential to knowing the Bible is to read the Bible. I mentioned earlier Dr. Townsend, the Shakespeare scholar. One morning a student said to him,

"Doctor, how can you know Shakespeare?" He answered, "Read Shakespeare." How are you going to know the Bible? Read the Bible, if you please. Read it!

How much time do you spend reading the Bible compared to the newspaper? How much time do you really spend in it? May I say, you ought to read it, in fact, several times. If you read a passage of Scripture and don't understand it, then read it again. And again and again. Keep praying about it and reading it, and you'll be amazed how the Spirit of God will open that passage to you. You have to read it; there's no substitute for that.

There is a very interesting incident in the Book of Nehemiah:

> *Now all the people gathered together as one man in the open square that was in front of the Water Gate; and they told Ezra the scribe to bring the Book of the Law of Moses, which the LORD had commanded Israel. So Ezra the priest brought the Law before the assembly of men and women and all who could hear with understanding on the first day of the seventh month. Then he read from it in the open square that was in front of the Water Gate from morning until midday, before the men and women and those who could understand; and the ears of all the people were attentive to the Book of the Law.* (Nehemiah 8:1–3 NKJV)

This is a very remarkable passage of Scripture. You see, the Jews had been in Babylonian captivity seventy years; many of them had never heard the Word of God. It did not circulate much in that day. There were not a hundred different translations abroad nor new ones coming off the press all the time. Probably there were just one or two copies in existence, and Ezra had one of those copies.

> *So they read distinctly from the book, in the Law of God; and they gave the sense, and helped them to understand the reading.* (Nehemiah 8:8 NKJV)

From the way the account is given, I assume that men of the tribe of Levi were stationed in certain areas among the people. After Ezra read a certain portion, he would stop to give the people who had listened an opportunity to ask questions of the men who were stationed out there to explain the Bible to them—"and the Levites . . . helped the people to understand the Law; and the people stood in their place" (Nehemiah 8:7 NKJV). Not only did they read the Word, but they caused the people to understand it.

I find that the people who are more ignorant of the Bible than anyone else are church members. They simply do not know the Word of God. It has been years since it has been taught in the average church. We need to get into the Word of God—not just reading a few favorite verses, but reading the entire Word of God. That is the only way we are going to know it, friend. That is God's method.

The third principle is a simple one: study the Bible. Someone came to Dr. G. Campbell Morgan years ago and said, "You speak as if you were inspired." Dr. Morgan replied,

"Inspiration is 95 percent perspiration." A fellow student in a Bible class I had in college said to our professor, "Doctor, that was dry reading you gave us." The professor said to him, "Then dampen it a little with the sweat of your brow." There are a lot of Christians who carry a Bible with the cover worn out, but they never wear out their minds or hearts studying it.

This is one of the reasons why I think the family altar can become a menace and a danger. I have been in homes where they gather at the table of a morning to read the daily devotional together, and boy, do they rush through it. That type of thing brings the Bible into disrepute. Did you ever hear of anybody learning trigonometry by reading two or three pages before going to bed at night?

When I was a teacher, I used to have these pious students who would say, "Well, now that you say the Spirit of God is our teacher, we are going to let Him speak to us." I had the feeling that some of them believed they could put their Bibles under their pillows at night and as they slept the names of the kings of Israel and Judah would come up through the duck feathers! Believe me, it won't come up through the duck feathers.

We have to knuckle down and study the Word of God. The Spirit of God will reveal truth to you, but any fact that you can dig out by using your brain, He won't reveal to you at all. I do not think He is revealing the truth to lazy people. We need people today who are willing to study the Word of God.

Next, meditate on the Bible. That's something that's gone out of style, but it's something that God taught His people. What does it really mean to meditate on the Word of God? There is a very interesting statement over in the first Psalm:

> *Blessed is the man who walks not in the counsel of the ungodly, nor stands in the path of sinners, nor sits in the seat of the scornful; but his delight is in the law of the LORD, and in His law he meditates day and night.* (Psalm 1:1–2 NKJV)

To meditate is to ruminate, to bring to mind, and to consider over and over. Ruminating is what a cow is doing when she chews her cud. The old cow goes out of a morning, and while the grass is fresh with dew she grazes. Then when the sun comes up and the weather is hot, the cow lies down under a tree, or stands there in the shade. You see her and you wonder what in the world that cow is chewing. She will chew there for an hour or two. She is meditating, friend. She is bringing the grass she ate of a morning (we are told that a cow has a complex stomach) out of one chamber and is transferring it to another. In the process, she is going over it again, chewing it up good.

You and I need to learn to do that in our thought processes. We are to get the Word of God, read it, have it out where we can look at it, then think about it, meditate on it.

I want to give one more: pass the Bible on to others. God has told us, "You shall be witnesses" (Acts 1:8 NKJV). He did not say that we should be scholars, walking encyclopedias, or memory books.

Someone has said that education is a process by which

information in the professor's notebook is transferred to the student's notebook, without passing through the mind of either. Well, there is a great deal of Bible truth like that. It is not practiced, not shared. We have been called to be witnesses today; therefore, we ought to pass it on to others.

I learned this lesson when I was in seminary. I pastored a little church, as did five other fellows, and we found that when we graduated, we were at least a year ahead of the other members of the class in our understanding of the Scriptures. Why? Because we were smarter than the others? No. Because we were passing it on. God was able to funnel into us a great deal more than He might have otherwise.

I think one of the grave dangers of a Bible class is of taking it in and not giving it out. God gave an illustration of that in the promised land itself. There are two seas, the Sea of Galilee and the Dead Sea. The Sea of Galilee is below sea level, but it's fresh water—why? It has an inlet, but it also has an outlet. But the Dead Sea has only an inlet. It has been taking in for literally millions of years, and it's never given out. It's dead.

It's amazing what giving out the Word of God will do for you. Why? Because the Spirit has a way of not communicating to us if we don't act upon the truth that we already have. When we act upon that truth, then He's prepared to give us more truth, you see. If we're giving out, then He'll begin to push in.

I believe that if these very simple rules were followed, it would revolutionize the lives of believers and our churches today. We are living in a day when the inspiration of the

Scripture is denied, but there is, to my judgment, no middle ground. Either you accept it as the infallible Word of God, or it is not the Word of God. And the Bible makes it very clear in that connection. For instance, "This Scripture had to be fulfilled, which the Holy Spirit spoke before by the mouth of David concerning Judas" (Acts 1:16 NKJV), and then "Therefore, as the Holy Spirit says: 'Today, if you will hear His voice'" (Hebrews 3:7 NKJV), and "The Spirit of the LORD spoke by me, and His word was on my tongue" (2 Samuel 23:2 NKJV).

Friend, may I say very candidly, you can't read definite and specific language like that and then turn around and say you don't believe it's the infallible Word of God. Either the Bible is the Word of God to you or it's not the Word of God to you. Either God said this or He didn't. You see, the Word itself puts you on the horns of a dilemma. God won't let you take a compromised position, and yet there are those today who attempt to do that.

Hebrews 1:1 (NKJV) says, "God, who at various times and in various ways spoke in time past to the fathers by the prophets." How clear that is—God spoke. Over and over in the Old Testament we're told "God said" or "the word of the Lord came." In fact, it's monotonous. Why is it repeated so often? Because God knew that in our day there'd be somebody who'd say He didn't say it, and God wanted to make it very clear that He did say it. You can accept it or you can leave it.

This is a day when God's words are being despised—rejected by the unbeliever and ignored by the believer. But listen to what the Word of God has to say concerning these words:

> *The words of the LORD are pure words, like silver tried in a furnace of earth, purified seven times.* (Psalm 12:6 NKJV)

These words are pure, tried like silver in the fire. If you cut these words, they bleed. It's the living Word of God, if you please, and "the law of the LORD is perfect" (Psalm 19:7 NKJV)—that means complete.

> *The law of the LORD is perfect, converting the soul; the testimony of the LORD is sure, making wise the simple; the statutes of the LORD are right, rejoicing the heart; the commandment of the LORD is pure, enlightening the eyes; the fear of the LORD is clean, enduring forever; the judgments of the LORD are true and righteous altogether.* (Psalm 19:7–9 NKJV)

What a testimony! May I say to you, this is the inviolate Word of God, authored by the Holy Spirit, and these pure, valuable, powerful words can convert the soul of man today.

Chapter 4

THE HOLY SPIRIT IN THE LIFE OF JESUS

I'd like to begin with a passage of Scripture that's ordinarily read only at Christmastime. It's found in the first chapter of the Gospel of Luke:

> *Now in the sixth month the angel Gabriel was sent by God to a city of Galilee named Nazareth, to a virgin betrothed to a man whose name was Joseph, of the house of David. The virgin's name was Mary. And having come in, the angel said to her, "Rejoice, highly favored one, the Lord is with you; blessed are you among women* [not *above* women, but *among* women]*!" But when she saw him, she was troubled at his saying, and considered what manner of greeting this was. Then the angel said to her, "Do not be afraid, Mary, for you have found favor with God. And behold, you will conceive in your womb and*

bring forth a Son, and shall call His name JESUS. He will be great, and will be called the Son of the Highest; and the Lord God will give Him the throne of His father David. And He will reign over the house of Jacob forever, and of His kingdom there will be no end." Then Mary said to the angel, "How can this be, since I do not know a man?" And the angel answered and said to her, "The Holy Spirit will come upon you, and the power of the Highest will overshadow you; therefore, also, that Holy One who is to be born will be called the Son of God."
(Luke 1:26–35 NKJV)

You may be scratching your head, wondering whether or not this is a Christmas sermon. Well, I begin here for the very simple reason that a primary, if not *the* primary, work of the Holy Spirit in connection with the Lord Jesus Christ was the conception of His humanity. The birth of the Lord Jesus Christ in His humanity was by the Holy Spirit. Actually, the dominance of the Holy Spirit in the earthly life of our Lord Jesus Christ is amazing. In fact, it's startling when you begin to lift out these passages and see what a dominant part the Holy Spirit of God played in His earthly life, all the way from the cradle to the grave.

But there is a great mystery about the virgin birth of Christ. Perhaps you have always just accepted it, but I'd like to raise several questions and maybe together we'll be able to find satisfactory answers. One of the questions is this: was the actual human body of the Lord Jesus a product of generation or creation? I have a notion that may be a question that has never crossed your mind before. Another question is this: was Adam's sin imputed to the Lord Jesus Christ at His birth? In other words, was the humanity of the Lord Jesus Christ sinless, or was it sanctified?

In order to answer those questions, we need to look at the operation of the Holy Spirit in the creation (I use that term advisedly) of the humanity of the Lord Jesus Christ. We have already read Dr. Luke's account of the virgin birth of Christ. Dr. Luke used more medical terms than Hippocrates, the father of medicine. Luke was a medical doctor of that day, and he was probably Greek. He certainly knew Greek culture, art, literature, and science well. So when he wrote about the virgin birth of the Lord Jesus, he wrote more in detail and as a doctor would write—unabashedly and unashamedly. "The Holy Spirit will come upon you, and the power of the Highest will overshadow you; therefore, also, that Holy One who is to be born will be called the Son of God." That statement is beyond human understanding. We can accept it, but I do not believe we can understand it.

Matthew confirmed the statement in his Gospel record:

Now the birth of Jesus Christ was as follows: After His mother Mary was betrothed to Joseph, before they came together, she was found with child of the Holy Spirit . . . But while he [Joseph] thought about these things, behold, an angel of the Lord appeared to him in a dream, saying, "Joseph, son of David, do not be afraid to take to you Mary your wife, for that which is conceived in her is of

> *the Holy Spirit. And she will bring forth a Son, and you*
> *shall call His name JESUS, for He will save His people*
> *from their sins."* (Matthew 1:18, 20–21 NKJV)

His humanity was conceived by the Holy Spirit, so the conception of the Lord Jesus Christ was supernatural.

The birth of Christ in Bethlehem, however, was normal and natural. So often we hear people emphasizing the virgin birth in Bethlehem, but, may I say to you, the miracle took place in Nazareth. It was there that He was conceived by the Holy Ghost. His birth nine months later in Bethlehem was as natural and normal as that of any other child—the Word of God makes that clear.

But the conception of the Lord Jesus was different: He was a creation of the Holy Spirit in the womb of a virgin, Mary. Just as the Holy Spirit hovered over the creation that was marred and brought something new, just as He moves into the heart of a darkened lost sinner and brings life and light, He moved in the womb of the virgin Mary and conceived there the humanity of the Lord Jesus Christ.

And that humanity, if you please, was holy and sinless. A human soul was conceived, and He was perfectly human. But at the same time, my beloved, He was God. He was perfectly human, but He was not any less God because He was man. And He was not any more man because He was God. He was a perfect man with a human body, a human soul, and a human spirit that was conceived by the Holy Spirit in the womb of the virgin Mary.

Now perhaps you're thinking, *Go on and explain that,*

McGee. The Word of God tells of four separate and different creations. We have, first of all, the creation of the first man by God. That was the work of the Holy Spirit taking the dust of the ground (that which was already made) and breathing life into it. That is how Adam came into existence (see Genesis 2:7). A man once said to me, "You know, man's been on this earth several hundred thousand years." I told him I agreed, so he said, "I didn't think you agreed with me. I thought you believed in the Genesis account." I answered, "I do, but the dirt out of which he was made was here a long time!" There has been no other man made in the way that Adam was made; he's unique. That was one method God had of creating.

Then He brought women into the world by taking a rib out of the side of Adam. As a preacher friend of mine said, "The Lord practiced with the man, because He saw the mistakes He'd made with man and He corrected them in the woman." (That's the reason why you women are so much better looking than we men!) But may I say to you, when the rib was taken from man to form woman, that was a unique operation; there's never been another like it (see Genesis 2:21–22).

Beginning at that time, God used His third method of creation: natural reproduction. We call it "natural" because one's born every minute, but I challenge any person to explain the natural birth. How can one of those little bitty fellas have in him all of the characteristics of the father or mother? We accept it, because we see it every day. But may I say to you, the birth of every child into this world is a glorious, wonderful miracle.

There is a fourth way God has of bringing men into this

world, and that was through the virgin birth of the Lord Jesus Christ. He brought into the world the humanity, the soul, and the spirit of our Lord, and the Holy Spirit was the Creator. May I say to you, the creation of a new human life is an inscrutable process. I do not propose to know any more about the processes involved in the creation of Jesus' humanity in Mary's womb than I do the original creation of man or natural creation today. The process by which the Lord Jesus was brought into this world, a man, is a great mystery.

But we know this: He was a true man "in all points tempted as we are, yet without sin" (Hebrews 4:15 NKJV). He knew no sin; He was "a lamb without blemish and without spot" (1 Peter 1:19 NKJV). He was "holy, harmless, undefiled, separate from sinners" (Hebrews 7:26 NKJV). It was His miraculous conception that made Him that way, my beloved. That's the reason He is different: it is the work of the Holy Spirit in Him.

Let us move on to another incident in the life of the Lord Jesus, and that is His baptism. To me, this was one of the greatest moments in His life.

Then Jesus came from Galilee to John at the Jordan to be baptized by him. And John tried to prevent Him, saying, "I need to be baptized by You, and You are coming to me?" [The humility of John the Baptist is an amazing thing. This man's attitude was, "He must increase; I must decrease."] *But Jesus answered and said to him, "Permit it to be so now, for thus it is fitting for us to fulfill all righteousness." Then he allowed Him.* (Matthew 3:13–15 NKJV)

Why was Jesus baptized? There may be several answers, but the primary reason is stated right here: "For thus it is fitting for us to fulfill all righteousness." Jesus was identifying Himself *completely* with sinful mankind. Isaiah had prophesied that He would be numbered with the transgressors (see Isaiah 53:12). Here was a king who identified Himself with His subjects.

Baptism means identification, and I believe identification was the primary purpose for the baptism of the Lord Jesus. He was not baptized to set an example for us; it was not a pattern for us to follow. Christ was holy—He did not need to repent, but you and I *do* need to repent. He was baptized to completely identify Himself with humanity.

But that was not the amazing thing. Let's read on:

> *When He had been baptized, Jesus came up immediately from the water; and behold, the heavens were opened to Him, and He saw the Spirit of God descending like a dove and alighting upon Him. And suddenly a voice came from heaven, saying, "This is My beloved Son, in whom I am well pleased."* (Matthew 3:16–17 NKJV)

Here we have a manifestation of the Trinity. As the Lord Jesus came out of the water, the Spirit of God descended upon Him like a dove, and the Father spoke from heaven: "This is My beloved Son, in whom I am well pleased." The Lord Jesus was then identified with His people. Oh, what a king He is!

But the thing I love is that the Holy Spirit came upon

Him like a dove. We looked at this in an earlier chapter, but I want to draw this illustration out again. Noah was in that ark for five months, and I bet he looked out every day and said, "My, when in the world is the water going to go down so I can get out of this place?" In order to get out just as soon as he could, he sent out two birds—a raven and a dove. The raven, black bird that it is, likes to eat dead things. It didn't come back—do you know why? Because that raven found a dead carcass floating on the water, so he stayed for a picnic. But the dove returned to the ark. Do you know why? Because it didn't find any place to light. Oh, there was a lot of refuse to land on, but he couldn't touch that. There wasn't a clean thing in the world for him to light on, so he came back to the safety of the ark.

That ark represents Christ and the Holy Spirit came upon Him like a dove because only on Him could the Holy Spirit find rest in fullness. Today we speak so glibly about being indwelt by the Holy Spirit. Did you know Christ had to die in order that the Holy Spirit might come? The Holy Spirit couldn't have gotten within twenty feet of us, if Christ had not died. You see, He died not only for our sins, but He died that the Holy Spirit might come in and indwell believers. It was only on Him that the Holy Spirit could come down like a dove.

The next tremendous work of the Holy Spirit in the life of Jesus came at the temptation of our Lord.

Then Jesus, being filled with the Holy Spirit, returned from the Jordan and was led by the Spirit into the wilder-

ness, being tempted for forty days by the devil. And in those days He ate nothing, and afterward, when they had ended, He was hungry. (Luke 4:1–2 NKJV)

There is a frightful and fearful darkness about the temptation of our Lord that is an appalling enigma. I must confess that I cannot explain it, but I will take you to the very edge, and at the fringe I hope we can learn something. There were unseen and hidden forces of evil all about Him. He was surrounded by powers of darkness and destruction. He grappled with the basic problems of mankind, that which is earthly, and He won a victory for mankind.

There are several preliminary considerations we need to have in mind as we look at the testing of our Lord. We are told that He was filled with the Holy Spirit. As man, the Son of God needed to be filled with the Spirit in order to meet the temptation. And, friend, *I* cannot face the temptations of this world in my own strength. In Romans 7:21 (NKJV) Paul told us, "I find then a law, that evil is present with me, the one who wills to do good." Haven't you found that to be true? Paul continued:

For what the law could not do in that it was weak through the flesh, God did by sending His own Son in the likeness of sinful flesh, on the account of sin: He condemned sin in the flesh, that the righteous requirement of the law might be fulfilled in us who do not walk according to the flesh but according to the Spirit. (Romans 8:3–4 NKJV)

Paul concluded that thought with: "I say then: Walk in the Spirit, and you shall not fulfill the lust of the flesh" (Galatians 5:16 NKJV). We *need* the Holy Spirit. Likewise, Jesus, in His humanity, needed the sustaining power of the Holy Spirit.

Everything He did, here as a man, He did in the power of the Holy Spirit. When He began His ministry, He taught by the power of the Holy Spirit, and He performed miracles by the power of the Holy Spirit. He—God in the flesh— even made this interesting statement: "I can of Myself do nothing" (John 5:30 NKJV). That ought to be a lesson for us.

What about His death and resurrection? Was the Spirit in control of them as well? May I say to you that when He died upon the cross, He died by the power of the Holy Spirit. Notice this very carefully:

> *How much more shall the blood of Christ,* who through the eternal Spirit offered Himself *without spot to God . . .* (Hebrews 9:14 NKJV, emphasis mine)

The Holy Spirit was upon Him when He went yonder to the cross, and our Lord offered Himself by the Holy Spirit. He did not die on the cross reluctantly, but rather "for the joy that was set before Him endured the cross" (Hebrews 12:2 NKJV). If He had not done so willingly and voluntarily, His sacrifice for you and me would have availed nothing. But He offered Himself willingly and gladly upon the cross by the eternal Spirit.

Before moving on, let's examine one more thing in relation to the role of the Spirit in the death of Christ.

This is He who came by water and blood—Jesus Christ;
not only by water, but by water and blood. And it is the
Spirit who bears witness, because the Spirit is truth. (1
John 5:6 NKJV)

You will recall that at the crucifixion of Jesus, His bones
were not broken in fulfillment of Scripture. In order to hasten death, the Romans would sometimes break the legs of
those who were hanging on the crosses, but John told us in
his Gospel:

But when they came to Jesus and saw that He was
already dead, they did not break His legs. But one of
the soldiers pierced His side with a spear, and immedi-
ately blood and water came out. And he who has seen
has testified, and his testimony is true; and he knows
that he is telling the truth, so that you may believe.
(John 19:33–35 NKJV)

John was present at the crucifixion of Christ, and he noted
something that no one else noted: when the soldier pushed
the spear into the side of Christ, there came out blood and
water—not just one element, but both elements. Water
speaks of what? Here it speaks of the Word of God. The
Lord Jesus said to Nicodemus, "Unless one is born of water
and the Spirit, he cannot enter the kingdom of God" (John
3:5 NKJV). The water is the living Word applied by the Spirit
of God. "He who came by water" in 1 John is the Word of
God that the Spirit of God uses. And the blood refers to the

death of Christ: "Jesus Christ; not only by water, but by water and blood" (1 John 5:6 NKJV).

It is the Spirit who can make these truths live. May I make this rather startling statement: the Lord Jesus told the disciples that between His death and resurrection and the Day of Pentecost they were to tarry in Jerusalem and to do nothing—they were *not* to witness.

> *Behold, I send the Promise of My Father upon you; but tarry in the city of Jerusalem until you are endued with power from on high.* (Luke 24:49 NKJV)

Why were they told to tarry in Jerusalem? Because they could not witness effectively without the Holy Spirit. Therefore, if anyone is to be saved, not only is Christ's redemptive death essential, but also that the Spirit of God is at work in hearts and lives.

I am encouraged by letters from listeners to our Bible-teaching radio broadcasts because they demonstrate that the Word of God taken by the Spirit of God can apply the blood of Christ to hearts and lives. Christ died for our sins, but the Spirit of God must make that real to us. Only the Spirit of God can make the death and resurrection of Christ real to you, for "it is the Spirit who bears witness, because the Spirit is truth" (1 John 5:6 NKJV).

His resurrection from the dead, also, was by the Holy Spirit.

> *But if the Spirit of Him who raised Jesus from the dead dwells in you, He who raised Christ from the dead will*

also give life to your mortal bodies through His Spirit who dwells in you. (Romans 8:11 NKJV)

Only the Holy Spirit of God could have raised that dead body from Joseph's tomb, and it is also the power of the Holy Spirit that reveals this truth to us.

I believe this is all very important. I've hit only the highlights of this tremendous subject, but here is what I've been trying to get to: if the Lord Jesus Christ in His humanity needed the Holy Spirit, what about you and me? If He needed the Holy Spirit, do you think that you are able to make it without the Holy Spirit in your life? I say to you, you won't make it. Friends, we need today that power that brought Christ back from the dead!

Paul prayed for the Ephesians:

That the God of our Lord Jesus Christ, the Father of glory, may give to you the spirit of wisdom [the Holy Spirit] *and revelation in the knowledge of Him, the eyes of your understanding being enlightened; that you may know . . . the exceeding greatness of His power toward us who believe, according to the working of His mighty power which He worked in Christ when He raised Him from the dead.* (Ephesians 1:17–20 NKJV)

What power was that? It was the power of the Holy Spirit, for Christ was raised by the power of the Holy Spirit. Paul's prayer was that this same power would work within each of us.

More than two thousand years ago, the Lord Jesus Christ was raised from the dead and taken back to the Father's right hand. That's the power of the Holy Spirit! If the Lord Jesus needed the power of the Holy Spirit, then surely you and I need it today. Are you trying to do it alone? Christianity to a great many people today is a do-it-yourself kit. But may I say to you that God has done all the work for you. When the Lord Jesus said, "It is finished!" yonder on the cross, your redemption was complete (John 19:30 NKJV). Not only was your redemption complete, but He made a way whereby you and I in our weakness, in our stumbling, and our sin can come to Him to receive forgiveness, be empowered by the Holy Spirit, be strengthened, and be helped.

Oh, what is your life? Is it just a miserable front? And back beneath that front, is there failure? Friend, why not let the Holy Spirit of God move in? *Then* you can live for God.

Chapter 5

WHAT *REALLY* HAPPENED ON THE DAY OF PENTECOST?

There is a great confusion and diversification of opinions when it comes to discussing the events that took place on the Day of Pentecost. What exactly did happen? In order to get the correct answer, let us look very carefully at the only record we are given of what actually occurred on that day. It will be necessary for us to move back and see the preparation that was made for the Day of Pentecost, because in God's plan and program, it was vitally important.

The Word of God is filled with paradoxes, and I believe we can gain a great deal of enlightenment on this particular subject by considering one of these seeming contradictions. Dr. Luke presented it when he was concluding his Gospel. He recorded these words of our Lord:

Thus it is written, and thus it was necessary for the Christ to suffer and to rise from the dead the third day, and that repentance and remission of sins should be preached in His name to all nations, beginning at Jerusalem. And you are witnesses of these things. (Luke 24:46–48 NKJV)

Then Jesus went on to tell them that they were to go into all the world and preach the gospel. He said they would receive power after the Holy Spirit came upon them, and He even marked out the steps, beginning at Jerusalem.

But then in the Book of Acts, Dr. Luke recorded another command of our Lord, which certainly sounds like a contradiction:

And being assembled together with them, [Jesus] *commanded them not to depart from Jerusalem, but to wait for the Promise of the Father, "which," He said, "you have heard from Me."* (Acts 1:4 NKJV)

In one place He said, "You should go out, beginning at Jerusalem," then shortly after that He said, "Wait. Don't go!" What did He mean? Well, may I suggest that these men had the facts, but they were to wait. Why? They were to wait, of course, for *power*. And the two statements present, not a contradiction, but a paradox.

Perhaps an illustration of what a paradox is would be in order. I was recently involved in a very good example. A pastor was giving me directions on how to reach his church, where I was to speak. He told me, "You drive out the freeway and turn off at Reid Avenue." And then he said, "You go right to go left."

I shook my head and said, "Come again?"

He said, "You have to go right in order to go left."

"Well," I said, "if we're going to go left, let's go left. Let's not fool with this right business."

He explained patiently, "You can't turn left because there are several lanes of oncoming traffic to your left. But you can pull off to the right at Reid Avenue, and then you'll come up over an overpass to go left, above the freeway. You go *right* to go *left*." That is not a contradiction on modern freeways—it's a paradox, if you please.

God said *go*, then He said *wait*, and then He said *go*. On every downtown street corner there is a paradox, for street lights represent a paradox. They say *go* and they say *stop*; but they don't do it at the same time. There is a moment that you are to stop and wait; there is a moment that you are to go.

But now will you notice that we have a further complication here in what our Lord said to His disciples after His resurrection:

> So Jesus said to them again, "Peace to you! As the Father has sent Me, I also send you." And when He had said this, He breathed on them, and said to them, "Receive the Holy Spirit." (John 20:21–22 NKJV)

You recall that Jesus had once said to them, "If you then, being evil, know how to give good gifts to your children, how much more will your heavenly Father give the Holy Spirit to those who ask Him!" (Luke 11:13 NKJV).

These men were taken aback! They had never heard of the Holy Spirit being given to sinners—so they had never asked for Him, as far as the record shows. But after His resurrection, in that interval between His resurrection and the Day of Pentecost, Jesus said, breathing upon them, "Receive the Holy Spirit." That was merely a temporary arrangement that was never to be repeated, just as many of the occurrences during that transition period will not bear repetition. These men, therefore, were born again before the Day of Pentecost.

But what *really* happened on the Day of Pentecost? I want to examine this subject from three different vantage points:

Wait for the Holy Spirit.

Want the Holy Spirit.

Witness in the power of the Holy Spirit.

WAIT FOR THE HOLY SPIRIT

The events leading up to the Day of Pentecost were all-important, for Pentecost was the "Bethlehem" of the Holy Spirit. On the Day of Pentecost, the Holy Spirit became incarnate in a body of believers. Of those who were present that day and heard the message of the gospel for the first time, three thousand were converted. They were born again and became the tabernacle, the temple, for the Holy Spirit. Simultaneously and instantaneously, they were placed into the body of believers by the baptism of the Holy Spirit. Listen to our Lord:

> *For John truly baptized with water, but you shall be baptized with the Holy Spirit not many days from now.* (Acts 1:5 NKJV)

The baptism of the Holy Spirit put them into the body of believers called the church. Paul said to the Corinthians,

> *For by one Spirit we were all baptized into one body—whether Jews or Greeks, whether slaves or free—and have all been made to drink into one Spirit.* (1 Corinthians 12:13 NKJV)

It doesn't make any difference who you are—if you trust Christ as your Savior, you are born again. The Holy Spirit identifies you, putting you into the body of believers, making you a member of the body of Christ, so that you are now identified with Christ. We will discuss that in more detail later, but the thing to note now is that on the Day of Pentecost, the church became the dwelling place for the Holy Spirit.

That is exactly what Paul wrote to the Ephesian believers:

> *In whom the whole building, being fitted together, grows into a holy temple in the Lord, in whom you also are being built together for a dwelling place of God in the Spirit.* (Ephesians 2:21–22 NKJV)

Today believers are the dwelling place of God through the Spirit.

Back in the Old Testament, God never did actually dwell in a temple. Solomon understood this. In his great dedicatory prayer, Solomon said,

> *But will God indeed dwell on the earth? Behold, heaven and the heaven of heavens cannot contain You. How much less this temple which I have built!* (1 Kings 8:27 NKJV)

Every instructed Israelite understood this also. For the first time in the history of the world, on the Day of Pentecost, God moved into a temple—a temple made up of individual believers who trusted Christ. Isn't that an amazing thing? They became the dwelling place of the Holy Spirit on the Day of Pentecost.

That work of the Holy Spirit on the Day of Pentecost was never repeated. It wasn't repeated any more than the birth of Christ was repeated. Having been born once, He does not have to be born again into the world. And, similarly, when the Holy Spirit came on the Day of Pentecost to begin the formation of the body of believers and take up His residence in them, He began a work that has never been repeated. In that sense, Pentecost cannot be duplicated.

Our Lord, after the Resurrection, was here for forty days in a vitally important postresurrection ministry. That is the reason He breathed upon His disciples, so that these men might understand the truth He was giving them in that day. But there was a ten-day wait for the Holy Spirit between

Christ's ascension and the descension of the Holy Spirit at Pentecost. For ten days the disciples were here alone upon this earth. There was, therefore, a brief period of waiting. That historic waiting period was never to be repeated.

You and I today do not have to wait for the Holy Spirit. He came nearly two thousand years ago at the Day of Pentecost, and nobody has had to wait for Him from that day to this.

This business today of waiting for the Holy Spirit reveals that a lot of folk have their geography mixed up. Jesus said to His disciples, "Wait in Jerusalem" (see Acts 1:4). He did not say to wait on Azusa Street; He said to wait in Jerusalem. And if you understand this to be a commandment for you, you need to go to Jerusalem to wait for Him. But, of course, neither the geography nor the waiting is needed today. Pentecost cannot, nor will it, be repeated or reenacted.

You do not, therefore, need a tarrying service. A great many people today are waiting for some great and sensational moving of the Holy Spirit. There was a man in my congregation who for years sat in front, waiting for some great emotional experience. He was a man with a very tender heart and sentimental nature. He was always waiting for a transforming experience that never came, even to his dying day. I used to tell him, "You don't have to depend on an experience. After all, an experience could be deceptive. You rest upon what God has said to you in His written Word."

There are all sorts of movements today called "revival." They are not revivals at all. A preacher up in northern California was telling me about visiting down here in southern California. He said he attended a certain church and later saw a delayed telecast of the service. On the television broad-cast, the preacher made an announcement that the place was packed out. This pastor told me, "Well, I was there and the place wasn't half full. I thought that was deception, so I got on the telephone and I called the preacher and said, 'Now I have just seen your television program and it was taped at the service I attended. You made the statement that the place was packed out. I was there—and it wasn't. How do you explain that?' The man replied, 'You poor, blind man! All of those seats you thought were empty were filled with angels.'"

Such foolishness is typical of the chicanery that is abroad today under the guise of revival. We are calling a great many things by their wrong names. There is no revival going on today in the church. There are a whole lot of pumped-up and trumped-up things *called* revivals, but there is no great moving of the Spirit of God in this land of ours. We hear of a real moving of the Spirit of God in a couple of other coun-tries, but not in ours.

Now, my beloved, although the Day of Pentecost can never be repeated, there is a waiting period in our lives before God can use us. We need that interlude, that waiting period of preparation. Paul the apostle had that period. After his conversion, you remember, the Lord Jesus said, "He is a chosen vessel of Mine to bear My name before Gentiles, kings, and the children of Israel" (Acts 9:15 NKJV). But before God was willing to send him out, He prepared that man for three years out yonder in the desert of Arabia (see Galatians 1:15–18). That is where God instructed him, and I think that is where the Lord taught him the lessons he later included in his Epistle to the Romans. There had to be that period of waiting, and you will find that during his entire ministry there were periods of waiting. In like manner, we need to wait for the Holy Spirit to direct and lead us.

Let me turn to one instance in the life of the apostle Paul. On his second missionary journey, we find him attempting to go into Bithynia, which in that day was well populated. Because they were having a population explosion in Bithynia, you would think that would be the place to go. But we read:

Now when they had gone through Phrygia and the region of Galatia, they were forbidden by the Holy Spirit to preach the word in Asia. After they had come to Mysia, they tried to go into Bithynia, but the Spirit did not per-mit them. (Acts 16:6–7 NKJV)

Paul made his first attempt to go into the province of Asia, where Ephesus was the capital. Actually there were quite a few cities in that region, and later on we learn of seven churches that came into existence (and there must have been twice that many); yet at this time he could not go there. So he tried Bithynia, but that door, too, was closed. The Holy Spirit left Paul only one direction to go, and that was west.

So passing by Mysia, they came down to Troas. (Acts 16:8 NKJV)

Paul arrived at Troas, but he did not know where to go from there. So he waited upon God. Then we read this:

And a vision appeared to Paul in the night. A man of Macedonia stood and pleaded with him, saying, "Come over to Macedonia and help us." Now after he had seen the vision, immediately we sought to go to Macedonia, concluding that the Lord had called us to preach the gospel to them. (Acts 16:9–10 NKJV)

Had you met Paul the apostle on the street in Troas that day and asked, "Paul, where are you going now?" he would have said, "I don't know." I know a lot of young people in training who can tell you exactly where they're going to be ten years in advance. I've heard them say in their testimonies, "God has called me to go to such-and-such a place." I don't believe a word of it. Apparently, God had not yet called Paul to go specifically to Europe. When he first arrived at Troas, he didn't know where he was to go next.

But had you met him on the street the following day, the puzzled look would have been gone. He would have explained, "I had a vision last night of a man of Macedonia who said, 'Come over and help us.' I interpret that to mean that God has called us to go to Europe." So off he went to Europe. That waiting period—waiting on the Holy Spirit for guidance—had ended.

We today are so busy attempting to do Christian work that we forget to wait on the Lord to make sure we are doing the thing *He* has called us to do. In these days of high technology and tension, we need periods of waiting before God. We even find it difficult to wait at the street corner when the light is red. We can't even wait for the light to change today, and yet God uses the stop-and-go method in our lives.

> But those who wait on the LORD shall renew their strength; they shall mount up with wings like eagles, they shall run and not be weary, they shall walk and not faint. (Isaiah 40:31 NKJV)

There is that period in our lives when we need to wait before God for strength.

WANT THE HOLY SPIRIT

The company in that upstairs room *wanted* the Holy Spirit.

> And when they had entered, they went up into the upper room where they were staying: Peter, James, John, and Andrew; Philip and Thomas; Bartholomew and Matthew; James the son of Alphaeus and Simon the Zealot; and Judas the son of James. These all continued with one accord in prayer and supplication, with the women and Mary the mother of Jesus, and with His brothers. (Acts 1:13–14 NKJV)

Here was this company of people who were following Jesus' instructions. How much they knew about what was going to happen on the Day of Pentecost is a matter of speculation. It is obvious that there was an air of anticipation, because our Lord, just before He ascended, had said,

But you shall receive power when the Holy Spirit has come upon you; and you shall be witnesses to Me in Jerusalem, and in all Judea and Samaria, and to the end of the earth. (Acts 1:8 NKJV)

They needed power to go against the pagan society of that massive Roman Empire upon which they would make such a tremendous impact, and they recognized their lack. There they were, so few in number, a small minority against the mob. They had no finances; they did not have any capital at all—and no church was sending them out. They did not have any buildings in those days (the church got along nicely without buildings for probably the first hundred years of its existence), and the church had no influence. These men were completely without prestige.

They were without all these things and, most of all, they were without Him. The Lord Jesus was gone. He had left them, and for ten days these men were alone—after three years of keeping company with Him. They had learned how to rest upon Him. They knew how dependent they were upon Him. And then there were those ten days of agonizing and waiting.

Jesus had said to them in the great Upper Room Discourse, "I will not leave you orphans; I will come to you" (John 14:18 NKJV). These folk, gathered yonder in that upper room, were waiting. Christ had promised to send the Holy Spirit, and they believed Him. They had high hopes and great expectations.

That period between the Ascension and Pentecost (those ten days when Christ was gone and the Holy Spirit had not come) was never to be repeated in the history of this world.

They had all the facts—they had been trained by Him for three years. Yet they had been warned, "Don't you dare venture out to witness to anybody." Why not get busy and take the gospel out? But He had said, "Wait." They wanted the Holy Spirit, and they were waiting.

Now, my beloved, there is a real sense in which every believer goes through a period of waiting and wanting. And during that period there is the setting of the sails for life. Decisions are made, habits are formed, directions are taken. I find that all the people God has used mightily have had in their lives that period of waiting and wanting. And may I say this to you, on the authority of the Word of God: every longing soul who is God's child and truly desires the will of God will be enabled to do His will. God will meet any eager and sincere soul who has this desire. When you say that He won't, you make God a liar. He says He will, and He will.

What we really want most of the time is our own way, and we want God to put His rubber stamp of approval on it. But He is not in the business of rubber-stamping anything. In fact, one thing God does not have is a rubber stamp. His will must be top priority for the believer.

Do you know why God stopped Saul of Tarsus on the Damascus road—why He arrested this one who hated Him, who persecuted Him, and who was the greatest enemy the church has ever had? Paul said that when the Lord appeared to him, He told him he would be sent to the Gentiles "to open their eyes, in order to turn them from darkness to light, and from the power of Satan to God, that they may receive forgiveness of sins and an inheritance among those who are sanctified by faith in Me" (Acts 26:18 NKJV). How did Paul respond? He said:

> *I was not disobedient to the heavenly vision.* (Acts 26:19 NKJV)

Any man who will be obedient, will find out God's will for his life; God says he will. Our trouble is that we have our own plans made. We have already bought our own ticket, and we are asking God to approve it. He will never do that. We must *want* the Holy Spirit in our lives.

WITNESS IN THE POWER OF THE HOLY SPIRIT

Now we come to the Day of Pentecost. What really happened?

> *When the Day of Pentecost had fully come, they were all with one accord in one place.* (Acts 2:1 NKJV)

Where was that place? Well, two places have been suggested. One is the upstairs room. Some assume that because they had met there for prayer, they were there again at this time. I personally do not think so. Then where were they? They were in a public place. To what public place would these men go? To the temple. And those at the temple witnessed something that had not been seen since the days of Solomon—the coming of the shekinah glory, not to the Holy of Holies, but into the hearts of frail, feeble men. That was Pentecost.

*And suddenly there came a sound from heaven, as of a
rushing mighty wind, and it filled the whole house where
they were sitting.* (Acts 2:2 NKJV)

It was not a wind; it was *like* a wind. It was an appeal to the
ear-gate.

*Then there appeared to them divided tongues, as of fire,
and one sat upon each of them.* (Acts 2:3 NKJV)

It was not the baptism of fire that so many say took place at
Pentecost. The baptism of fire is judgment, which is yet to
come—we read of that in the Book of Revelation. When the
wrath of God is revealed, fire will come from heaven. That,
my friend, is the baptism of fire. And if men will not have
the baptism of the Holy Spirit, they must have the other.
What came at Pentecost was not fire; but it was *as of* fire. It
appealed to the eye-gate, you see.

Now will you notice the most remarkable thing of all:

*And they were all filled with the Holy Spirit and began
to speak with other tongues, as the Spirit gave them utter-
ance.* (Acts 2:4 NKJV)

Were they baptized with the Holy Spirit? Notice—*it does not
say so.* It says they were *filled* with the Holy Spirit. This is
probably the most important thing one can say today when
there is so much wild theology on the doctrine of the Person
and work of the Holy Spirit.

Now somebody will ask, "But don't you think they were baptized?" I know they were; but, you see, the only thing that is recorded is the *experience* they had, and nobody experiences the baptism of the Holy Spirit. It happens, but it was not and is not an experience. He had baptized them, for you cannot be filled with the Holy Spirit until you have been baptized with the Holy Spirit. But the only experience they had on the Day of Pentecost was the filling with the Holy Spirit. Then they began to speak.

Nowhere will you find a commandment for any believer to be baptized with the Holy Spirit. The minute you trust Christ you *are* baptized, you are identified with Christ and put into the body of believers. You are not asked to do anything about it. You do not even have to know it. But, my beloved, you and I are given this command:

> **Do not be drunk with wine, in which is dissipation; but be filled with the Spirit.** (Ephesians 5:18 NKJV)

This is something that was repeated for these men again and again after the Day of Pentecost, because they needed constant filling.

These apostles of Christ were then filled with the Holy Spirit. Peter could stand up and preach in the power of the Spirit. They began to move out with the gospel, and the church started to spread to the ends of the earth. The church did not bog down until men went forth who were *not* filled with the Holy Spirit.

There is power today in *waiting*. There is purpose today in *wanting*. There is God's program today in *witnessing*—for that *is* His program.

Doing Christian work—going through Christian acts, performing Christian exercises—may be simply the expression of a religious zombie. But the filling of the Holy Spirit is essential for any service that God can honor. The Bible is a dead book to you unless you are filled with the Holy Spirit. Prayer is meaningless without a filling of the Holy Spirit. And your relationship with Christ Himself will become ashes unless the Spirit of God fills you, my beloved.

In my ministry, I meet many people who are going through the motions of Christianity—they don't do this, and they don't do that, and they wouldn't dream of doing the other thing. But their lives are vacuums, utterly lacking in the joy of the Lord. What's the matter with them? They are not filled with the Holy Spirit. They need a daily filling of the Holy Spirit of God. You can be regenerated, you can be indwelt, you can be baptized by the Spirit of God and still not be ready for service.

Such Christians are like Samson. Samson went forth after he got his hair cut (there was no strength in his hair; the strength was in the Holy Spirit)—"But he did not know that the LORD had departed from him" (Judges 16:20 NKJV). God have mercy on us. It can happen to us today. We can so toy and play with evil that there does come a time when the Holy Spirit is grieved, and we go forth in our own strength. Stephen said to the Sanhedrin, a religious body of the Jews:

You stiff-necked and uncircumcised in heart and ears!
You always resist the Holy Spirit; as your fathers did, so
do you. (Acts 7:51 NKJV)

You, today, do not need to seek for the Holy Spirit. If
you are a child of God, a believer, He indwells you. And you
need not seek the baptism of the Holy Spirit, for that was
accomplished when you trusted Christ. But I do believe that
if you and I are going to do anything for God today, we
must have a fresh infilling of the Holy Spirit. And, my
beloved, it is only as you and I yield to Him and our will
moves out of the way that the Spirit of God can move in and
bring God's will to bear in our lives.

I beseech you therefore, brethren, by the mercies of God,
that you present your bodies a living sacrifice, holy,
acceptable to God, which is your reasonable service.
(Romans 12:1 NKJV)

Wait upon God for His direction in serving. *Want* the
Holy Spirit to fill you for serving. *Witness* in obedience as
the Holy Spirit directs, fills, and empowers you.

May He fill us in the days that lie ahead as He filled and
empowered those men on the Day of Pentecost. Oh, how all
God's children need it!

Chapter 6

THE HOLY SPIRIT IN THE WORLD

Scripture clearly delineates seven unique and peculiar ministries that the Holy Spirit came to perform: He came in order that He might restrain evil in the world, convict of sin, regenerate, indwell, seal, baptize, and fill. Those are the seven ministries of the Holy Spirit in this present age. We will be dealing with them all throughout these pages, but now I want to examine the two ministries of the Spirit that are related specifically to the world: He restrains evil and convicts of sin.

HE RESTRAINS EVIL

We are told that the Holy Spirit is the restrainer of evil.

And now you know what is restraining, that he may be revealed in his own time. For the mystery of lawlessness is already at work; only He who now restrains will do so until He is taken out of the way. (2 Thessalonians 2:6–7 NKJV)

Paul was describing here what things must take place before the Lord can come to the earth. Now the restrainer of whom Paul spoke is obviously a person, but who restrains evil in the world? To answer that question, let's turn to another passage:

And the LORD said, "My Spirit shall not strive with man forever, for he is indeed flesh; yet his days shall be one hundred and twenty years." (Genesis 6:3 NKJV)

God was saying that the Spirit of God, even in the days of Noah, was striving in the world despite the great tide of evil that brought the Flood upon mankind. The Spirit of God even in that day was holding back (restraining) the judgment of the Flood.

Now not everyone agrees that 2 Thessalonians 2:6–7 refers to the Holy Spirit restraining evil in the world, but I think it does. But for the sake of argument, let's look at some of the other interpretations that have been given of this passage. I think our examination will throw light on the fact that the only reasonable interpretation is that the Holy Spirit is the restrainer of evil.

First, there have been very good men, competent men,

who have said that the church is the restrainer. Well, it's not the church. I have a very simple answer for that: the restrainer is a person, you see. It says very clearly, "Until *He* is taken out of the way." Whenever the church is referred to, it is always a she—she's a bride of Christ. So I feel that you can't under any circumstance say that the restrainer is the church. After all, does the church restrain evil? No! May I say the one thing the church should stand for under all circumstances is upholding the law. Yet many ministers have done the church a discredit for going with the forces of lawlessness. So it cannot be the church.

Second, there are those who would argue that the restrainer is Satan. Well, that would mean that he would be restraining himself, and he just wouldn't be doing that. That type of an argument, to my judgment, is not quite valid at all, and it just doesn't fit into the theme of Scripture.

Finally, there have been those who have said that the restrainer was the Roman government. It is true that the Roman government brought law and order, but does that qualify it as being the restrainer in the world? To tell the truth, the greatest advocate for law and order is going to be the Antichrist himself, that is, after he comes into power. You talk about regimentation—you won't be able to buy or sell in the Great Tribulation period without getting instructions from him and without having the mark of the Beast upon you. So, certainly, the Roman Empire's implication of laws can't qualify it as being the restrainer spoken of in 2 Thessalonians.

These, as far as I know, are the only arguments that have ever been brought forth to suggest the identity of the restrainer, and we cannot accept any of them. Only one explanation meets the requirement, and that is that the Holy Spirit came into the world on the Day of Pentecost and entered into a peculiar ministry, part of which is to restrain evil. Why? So that the gospel might go out.

You may remember that Paul said we are to pray that we might live "quiet and peaceable" lives (1 Timothy 2:2 NKJV). And why is that? It is so that the witness of the Word might go out to the ends of the earth. Therefore, the Holy Spirit is in the world, restraining evil, and enabling the believer to attain that peaceful life.

I say this reverently, but sometimes when you see the evil things that are happening in the world today, you may wonder if He is on the job! Is He really restraining evil? Well, let me say to you that the Spirit of God *is* restraining evil, and this world would be ten thousand times worse than it is if He were not here. It's amazing how bad man can become without any restraint put upon him at all.

That has happened several times in our history, when all restraint was removed. Back in 1919, the Boston police force went on strike. Some of the good people of Boston thought they could ignore it. I imagine they said, "We are civilized, cultured people here in Boston. We actually don't even need the police." May I say to you that by the time the sun went down that first day, they had called out the militia because of the vandalism and looting of the stores that was going on. Boston didn't really know how bad man could be until they didn't have policemen on the beat.

And, by the way, we ought to be thankful for our police

forces. I want to say that I appreciate the police except when one is following me while I'm driving. That's the one time I don't like them. But they restrain evil, and they restrain a great many of these speed demons as well! One day I got on the freeway and things were moving so slowly that I thought something must have happened to block it up. Do you know what it was? It was a policeman going along just as slow as can be, and everybody slowed down to his speed. Nobody dared go around. So the police do restrain evil.

You and I ought to be thankful for the restraining ministry of the Holy Spirit, because it has a benefit for us in the world today.

But what about when "He is taken out of the way" (2 Thessalonians 2:7 NKJV)? My friend, the Holy Spirit will be present in the world, but He will no longer restrain evil. The Holy Spirit came on the Day of Pentecost to perform a specific ministry of calling out a body of believers in the church, which is referred to as the body of Christ. When the church is removed from the earth, that peculiar ministry of the Holy Spirit will end. One of His ministries in this particular era has also been that of restraining evil. It is absolutely essential that He be a restrainer of evil in order for the gospel to penetrate a Satan-controlled and Satan-blinded world. The Holy Spirit will be in the world after the church is removed just as He was in the world before Pentecost.

In reading the Old Testament, you will find the Spirit of God working in the hearts and lives of men and women. Many multitudes were brought to God, but He was not restraining evil in the world, and He was not baptizing believers into the body of the church in the Old Testament. That is what He is doing today, but that ministry will cease. However, He will still be in the business of getting men and women to Christ. He will continue His ministry, which has always been one of taking God's creation and renovating it. The Spirit of God hovers over this earth today and will continue to do so after the church is removed from the earth. The only difference is that during the Great Tribulation Period, He will no longer be restraining evil.

He Convicts of Sin

The second ministry of the Spirit as it relates to the world is that He convicts the lost and also convicts the saved. The convicting work of the Holy Spirit is, to my judgment, the most ignored ministry of the Spirit of God. I say this very carefully, but I do want to say it: I believe the reason why so many unsaved people are in the church today is because they have never felt convicted. One of the saddest conditions of the church at present is the lack of conviction in the heart of even professing Christians regarding the sin in their lives. When was the last time you heard a saint say he was sorry? That he caused difficulty? Or that he did something wrong? The ones I've talked to are always making an excuse or justifying themselves. In fact, I've encountered some who make it out that I'm the one who's wrong!

In fact, I once knew a leader in a church who left his wife and ran off with another woman. Then he came to me and told me *I* was wrong because I'd said *he* was wrong. May I say, that man never had any conviction of sin, whatsoever. How many saints today say, "I'm wrong, I made a mistake"? I would say that one of the greatest needs we have today is the honest conviction of sin by the Holy Spirit of God.

Not only is this His ministry within the hearts of believers, but it is a ministry to the world as well.

> *For when Gentiles, who do not have the law, by nature do the things in the law, these, although not having the law, are a law to themselves, who show the work of the law written in their hearts, their conscience also bearing witness, and between themselves their thoughts accusing or else excusing them* [one another]. (Romans 2:14–15 NKJV)

That is a tremendous statement. Paul put down the basis on which God will judge good people. God can and will judge the heathen by His own conscience. Some folk think that because the heathen do not have the revelation of God, they will escape God's judgment. But the fact is that they are not living up to the light they have. God will judge them on that basis. Why? Because everyone has some sense of right and wrong. Where do we get it? Well, as we've said, the Holy Spirit is in the world to convict it. That's the reason why the psychologist can't help you get rid of your guilt complex—every man and woman has it, and the Spirit of God won't let you get rid of it.

Some missionary friends have told me about one of the tribes out in the Pacific that will eat human beings, just as a matter of course. In fact, that is the course—human being.

(Oh, I ought not to say those things. I'll try to be a little more serious.) But the missionary said that these people have a high sense of honesty—they never steal. You could take your billfold, put it out in the open, come back a week later, and it would still be there! If I left mine, I could understand why. But it would never be touched, because they will not steal.

But, on the other hand, they wouldn't mind eating their mother-in-law! We believe that you ought not to eat your mother-in-law, but stealing, well, it's a pretty common practice today. May I say to you, go off and think that over for a while. Who's right? Which is better, not to steal and eat your mother-in-law, or to steal and not eat your mother-in-law?

You can think that one over for a while, because there are some people who think they are right and we are wrong. But my point is that these people have an inherent sense of right or wrong, just as the writer to the Romans says, they "show the work of the law written in their hearts, their conscience also bearing witness."

Our Lord Jesus said:

> *Nevertheless I tell you the truth. It is to your advantage that I go away; for if I do not go away, the Helper* [the Holy Spirit] *will not come to you; but if I depart, I will send Him to you. And when He has come, He will convict the world of sin, and of righteousness, and of judgment.* (John 16:7–8 NKJV)

When the Holy Spirit is come, He will convict the world in the way a judge or a prosecuting attorney presents evidence to bring a conviction. The Spirit of God wants to present evidence in your heart and in my heart to bring us to a place of conviction, and that, of course, means a place of decision. There must be a conviction before we can turn in faith and trust to Jesus Christ.

In the present ministry of the Holy Spirit in the world, He will convict the world of three things: sin, righteousness, and judgment. Our Lord explains for us what that sin is: "Because they do not believe in Me" (John 16:9 NKJV). What is the greatest sin in the world? Murder? No. Who are the greatest sinners in this age? We've had some rascals, haven't we? Every age has. We might point out Hitler, or Stalin, or Karl Marx. Well, who is the greatest sinner today? I want to say to you very carefully that *you* could be the greatest sinner living today. The question is this: have you accepted Christ? Unbelief is a state and there is no remedy if you refuse to trust Christ. It is just as simple and important as that. This is a decision that every man must make. The man today who is rejecting Jesus Christ is, in the sight of God, the greatest sinner.

Secondly, the Holy Spirit will convict the world of righteousness. Jesus Christ was delivered for our offenses and raised again for our justification (see Romans 4:25). Jesus Christ returned to the Father because He had completed His work here. When He died on the cross, He died a judgment death. He took my guilt and your guilt and died in our place. He was delivered for our offenses, but He was raised for our justification. He was raised from the dead that you and I might not only have our sins subtracted, but so that we might have His righteousness added.

That is very important, because you and I need righteousness. It is not enough to have our sins forgiven. We cannot stand in God's presence if we are nothing more than pardoned criminals. Christ has made over to us *His* righteousness. That is the righteousness Paul spoke of: "that I may gain Christ, and be found in Him, not having my own righteousness, which is from the law, but that which is through faith in Christ, the righteousness which is from God by faith" (Philippians 3:8–9 NKJV). He not only subtracts our sin, but He adds His righteousness. If we are to have any standing before God, we must be in Christ, for He is our righteousness.

Thirdly, it is difficult for a great many believers to understand that we live in a judged world. One hears people say that they'll take their chances. They act as if they are on trial. My friend, you are not on trial. God has already declared you a lost sinner, and He has already judged you—"For the wages of sin is death, but the gift of God is eternal life in Christ Jesus our Lord" (Romans 6:23 NKJV). We live in a world that has already been judged and is like the man waiting in death row for his execution. The judgment against all of us is "Guilty" because all our righteousness is as filthy rags in the sight of God. If we had to stand before God in our own filthy rags, we would not only be ashamed of ourselves, but we would also see how guilty we are.

Today many people don't like to hear about judgment, and they resent it a great deal. The lost world hates many things about God: for instance, His omnipotence. They don't like the fact that it is His universe and He is running it His way. They don't like that God saves by grace and that man has already been declared lost.

Those are the three things of which the Holy Spirit convicts the world today. I think we should call attention to this: all who are saved must first be convicted. I do not believe you can be saved until you've been convicted. That's the reason why I keep talking about sin. Someone may say, "My, why don't you get on something else?" Well, I'll tell you why, because it's neglected by so many that I feel like someone needs to emphasize it. Until you and I come under a conviction of sin, there will be no conversion. There will be no turning to Christ. There must be conviction; it's essential.

That doesn't mean shedding of tears or some big emotional upheaval, although it may affect some like that. But it's an appeal to the highest part of man. My friend, until you can go to Christ and say to Him, "I'm guilty, and Christ bore my guilt," you can't pass from death to life. Can you say that? Do you believe that? Why do we bring people to Jesus, my friend? What is He? My friend, He is a Savior—a Savior who died on a cross because you and I are guilty, and until we believe that, we'll not come to Him.

But instead of conviction, we have a lot of nodding of heads today. There's no crying out to God! Let me ask you a question: when was the last time you wept over your sins? When did you last cry out to Him? You see, He'll convict the world but if you are His child, He will convict you personally, as well. All who are saved must first be convicted by the Holy Spirit.

There's another side to this: not all who are convicted are saved. The Word of God gives to us plenty of examples. One is the rich young ruler.

> *Now a certain ruler asked Him, saying, "Good Teacher, what shall I do to inherit eternal life?" So Jesus said to him, "Why do you call Me good? No one is good but One, that is, God. You know the commandments . . ." And he said, "All these things I have kept from my youth." So when Jesus heard these things, He said to him, "You still lack one thing. Sell all that you have and distribute to the poor, and you will have treasure in heaven; and come, follow Me." But when he heard this, he became very sorrowful, for he was very rich.* (Luke 18:18–23 NKJV)

He may have felt conviction, been sorrowful, and shed tears, but, my friend, he went away from Christ. Did he choose to follow the Lord later on? We hope so, but Scripture does not tell us.

There is another group of men, and they have always interested me a great deal. They are the men who tried Paul the apostle. Two of them were Felix and Agrippa. After Paul had presented to them his conversion and given them his testimony, Felix was interested.

> *Now as he reasoned about righteousness, self-control, and the judgment to come, Felix was afraid and answered, "Go away for now; when I have a convenient time, I will call for you."* (Acts 24:25 NKJV)

But he never had a convenient season. Here was a man who heard the Word of God, and the King James Version even says that he "trembled." He said, "Boy, I want to hear more about this. I'll call for you when I've got more time." But he never had time. He was under conviction, but he was never saved.

Then there was Agrippa who said to Paul, "You almost persuade me to become a Christian" (Acts 26:28 NKJV). He came under conviction, and it was *almost* enough to lead him to salvation, but not quite. May I say to you that there are many people who come under conviction but are never saved. They come under conviction, weep for a time over their sin, bemoan their condition, and yet they'll turn their backs on Christ and walk away. There's never real conviction, and therefore there's never real conversion.

The last one we'll turn to is the worst one of all, and that's Judas Iscariot. He was one of the most frightful men who ever crossed the pages of Scripture. Matthew gave us this record:

> *Then Judas, His betrayer, seeing that He had been condemned, was remorseful* [repented] *and brought back the thirty pieces of silver to the chief priests and elders, saying, "I have sinned by betraying innocent blood." And they said, "What is that to us? You see to it!" Then he threw down the pieces of silver in the temple and departed, and went and hanged himself.* (Matthew 27:3–5 NKJV)

For three years, Judas had been a phony and fooled everybody. There was never any real deep conviction in his heart as there was in Simon Peter who said, "You are the Christ, the Son of the living God" (Matthew 16:16 NKJV). Judas could say, "Master, Master," but he never could call Him "Lord." This man Judas kept up his front until finally the time came to betray Christ.

Now, I do not know what the thinking of his mind was, but there are several explanations. Those who have tried to make an excuse for him have even argued that Judas's purpose was to force Christ's hand. He didn't think Christ would go to the cross, but instead He'd just go straight to the throne. I don't believe that, but it's one of the explanations. I'd argue, instead, that Judas experienced no real conviction. When he met the chief priests in the temple, they were taking Jesus in for the final trial. So Jesus was right there in that company. Why didn't Judas fall down before Him right there, repent, and beg His forgiveness? He never did ask God's forgiveness. He was under conviction, but not a *real* conviction which would have led to his salvation. It actually led to his suicide.

May I say to you, many men and women have a conviction of the Holy Spirit, but it's not a conviction that leads to conversion. These are examples of it.

The Holy Spirit will convict the world of sin, of righteousness, and judgment. Yet, there comes a time when God says, "My Spirit shall not strive with man forever" (Genesis 6:3 NKJV). A man can keep rejecting and rejecting until finally God will do the rejecting. Take Pharaoh, for example—six times we are told that Pharaoh hardened his own heart, and then there came a day when God hardened his heart (see Exodus 7–11).

Friend, if you harden your heart against God, He will harden it as well. If you shut your eyes and won't listen, God will shut you out and be through with you. What does God have to do to be through with a man? May I say this: absolutely nothing. You can never be converted, my friend, unless the Spirit of God does it. Therefore, all God has to do is do nothing, and you are hardened.

You can't trifle with God. We are living in a day when He is ridiculed, and I'm confident that many people today have already stepped over the line and God is through with them. This is very solemn, my friend. You can go too far with God. The Holy Spirit is in the world today, but you can go to a place where He will no longer strive for you.

Chapter 7

THE HOLY SPIRIT
AND REGENERATION

There is a mystery, a wonder, and a glory about the work of the Spirit of God in the life of the believer. One such work of the Spirit is regeneration.

Let me begin by saying that most of us do not thoroughly appreciate our condition before regeneration. Notice the picture given in Scripture of the human family before regeneration:

> *And you He made alive, who were dead in trespasses and sins, in which you once walked according to the course of this world, according to the prince of the power of the air, the spirit who now works in the sons of disobedience, among whom also we all once conducted ourselves in the lusts of our flesh, fulfilling the desires of the flesh and of*

the mind, and were by nature children of wrath, just as the others. (Ephesians 2:1–3 NKJV)

That's God's picture of the human family. Before regeneration, when we are still lost sinners, we are absolutely dead to God in trespasses and sins. The lost man has no desire, no longing, no love for God. As far as God is concerned, he is dead.

Of course, it is not a physical death, but spiritual. Just as Adam was told, "But of the tree of the knowledge of good and evil you shall not eat, for in that day that you eat of it you shall surely die" (Genesis 2:17 NKJV). Man didn't die physically that day; it was almost a millennium after that before Adam and Eve died. But they did die spiritually that day. That is, they were dead to God.

"Having no hope and without God in the world" (Ephesians 2:12 NKJV) is the condition of every lost man today. That's the reason why we need to be regenerated, to be born again. We cannot pull ourselves up by our bootstraps. A great many people say, "If I could just do a little bit better, maybe be a little more religious." My friend, that's not what we need at all. What we need is to be born again. We need to be brought out of a state of death and into the state of life.

That, therefore, creates the necessity for regeneration, because the center of man's life needs to be changed. Even David, God's man, in the time of his sin cried out to God, "Create in me a clean heart, O God, and renew a steadfast spirit within me" (Psalm 51:10 NKJV).

I am confident that the Holy Spirit gave us one classic example within the pages of Scripture for the purpose of revealing to us His work of regeneration. The man who was chosen for this illustration was religious to his fingertips and manifested the kind of life that the Old Testament endorsed. He tithed, he always went to the temple, he fasted, he went through religious rituals—he did all of the outward things that were commanded. His name was Nicodemus, and as we examine his story, I will highlight the things that pertain to the regenerating work of the Holy Spirit.

There was a man of the Pharisees named Nicodemus, a ruler of the Jews. (John 3:1 NKJV)

That is the Holy Spirit's biography of the man, Nicodemus, and from it we learn three things. He was a man of the Pharisees, which means he belonged to the best group of people in Israel. They were conservative fundamentalists who believed the Word of God. Secondly, we learn that his name was Nicodemus. And, lastly, he was a ruler of the Jews. The Spirit of God did not accidentally pick this man to illustrate regeneration; he represented the very best of the Old Testament Jewish society.

This man came to Jesus by night and said to Him, "Rabbi, we [that is, Nicodemus and the other Pharisees] *know that You are a teacher come from God; for no one can do these signs* [miracles] *that You do unless God is with him."* (John 3:2 NKJV)

That was genuine flattery. Our Lord would have called him on it if it hadn't been sincere. Jesus didn't mind calling the Pharisees hypocrites when they deserved it (see Matthew 23:27), but Nicodemus was not a hypocrite. He was a good man. He was sincere, and he believed that Jesus was a prophet from God. He said very frankly, "No man could do the miracles that you are doing unless God is with him."

Actually, I think Nicodemus had quite a flattering speech prepared, but the Lord Jesus never let him get to it. He broke in and answered Nicodemus rather abruptly.

> *Jesus answered and said to him, "Most assuredly, I say to you, unless one is born again, he cannot see the kingdom of God."* (John 3:3 NKJV)

Why did Jesus bring up this matter of the kingdom of God? Nicodemus hadn't said anything about it—but he was going to, and our Lord headed him off. He intended to talk about the kingdom of God. I think Nicodemus's whole reason for coming to Jesus as a representative of the Pharisees was to talk to Him about the kingdom of God. But the Lord Jesus said, "You can't even see the kingdom of God until you've been born again." Nicodemus, as brilliant and religious as he was, was blind—not only dead in trespasses and sins, but blind, my beloved. That's why so much is said about Christ being the light, and to be born again means to have the light of Christ shine in on you, my friend. But Nicodemus, like many today, didn't have it.

Our Lord's response to him was, "Unless one is born

again." The Greek word for "again" is *anothen*, which means "from above." But Nicodemus couldn't think of anything but a physical birth:

> *Nicodemus said to Him, "How can a man be born when he is old? Can he enter a second time into his mother's womb and be born?"* (John 3:4 NKJV)

Our Lord wasn't speaking of a physical birth at all. He was speaking about a spiritual birth. But Nicodemus couldn't understand about a spiritual birth. The reason was that he had no spiritual capacity to comprehend it.

> *Jesus answered, "Most assuredly, I say to you, unless one is born of water and the Spirit, he cannot enter the kingdom of God."* (John 3:5 NKJV)

To be born from above means to be born of the Spirit of God, my beloved.

Let's turn to another passage that may be helpful to us as we attempt to understand this:

> *Who were born, not of blood, nor of the will of the flesh, nor of the will of man, but of God.* (John 1:13 NKJV)

John was speaking here about the fact that those who come to Christ are not born of blood. That is, it's not because they have a godly father or mother. It may be wonderful to be brought up in a Christian family, my friend, but that does not make you saved. Nor, he says, is it by the will of the flesh. That means you do not become a child of God through any effort on your part. Nor is it by the will of man, which means it's not by someone laying his hand upon you or putting you through a ceremony—those things never make you a child of God. Being born again means to be regenerated by the Holy Spirit of God—He must bring new life to the believer.

But there was poor Nicodemus asking, "How can a man be born when he is old?" I'm in entire sympathy with him. Here was this religious leader, and he hadn't any idea that Jesus was talking about a spiritual birth. It is a new birth "of water and the Spirit."

Now what does it mean to be born "of water and the Spirit"? There are those who think that to be born of water is a reference to water baptism. But this would be a strange expression if it did refer to that. Then, there have been several very fine Christian doctors who interpret "born of water" as the physical birth, which is a birth in water; that is, the child in the womb is in water. I don't think that is what is meant here at all. He wasn't talking about the difference between natural birth and spiritual birth, but He was talking about *how* a man could be born "from above" or "born again."

In my judgment, "water" here is the Word of God. Scripture makes it very clear. Later in the Gospel of John, Jesus says, "You are already clean because of the word which I have spoken to you" (John 15:3 NKJV). The Word of God is likened to water again and again. So I believe that "born of water and the Spirit" means that a person must be born again by the Holy Spirit's use of the Scripture. No one can be born again without the Word of God applied by the Spirit of God. One today is born from above by the use of water, which is the Word of God, and the Holy Spirit, making it real to the heart.

There are three outstanding conversions in the Book of Acts. They have been given to us, I think, primarily as illustrations. There is the conversion of the Ethiopian eunuch, the conversion of Cornelius, and the conversion of Paul. These three men are representations of the three families of Noah: the son of Shem, the son of Ham, and the son of Japheth. In each of their cases, the Word of God was used by the Spirit of God for their conversion. God's method seems to be the *Word* of God, used by the *Spirit* of God, given through a *man* of God. I am confident that our Lord, saying that one must be born of water and the Spirit, referred to the Spirit of God using the Word of God. Without this, Nicodemus could not enter the kingdom of God.

> *That which is born of the flesh is flesh, and that which is born of the Spirit is spirit.* (John 3:6 NKJV)

God has no plan, as I can see, to improve the old nature. This old nature is to end when we end our earthly career. It will go into the grave with us, and that will end it. But until then, you've got it, my friend. You'll never get rid of it in this life. That which is born of the flesh is flesh—God will not improve it. But that which is born of the Spirit is spirit, my beloved, and that is what happens when a lost, dead sinner becomes a child of God, born of—regenerated by—the Spirit.

Notice what our Lord said next:

> *Do not marvel that I said to you, "You must be born again." The wind blows where it wishes, and you hear the sound of it, but cannot tell where it comes from and where it goes. So is everyone who is born of the Spirit.* (John 3:7–8 NKJV)

The word translated here as "wind" is the Greek *pneuma*, which is the same word used for the Holy Spirit. Just as we can hear the sound of the wind blowing, we can see the working of the Holy Spirit. I like that comparison. Jesus was saying, "You can't tell where the wind comes from or where it is going." The air currents and winds are something that man still doesn't control. The wind blows where it wills. We can't detour it, and we can't change it. Although we can't control the wind, we surely can tell when it's blowing.

Now, friend, I don't know how to explain to you the spiritual birth. I know there are a lot of books being published that claim to explain it, but the difference between the authors and me is that they don't seem to know that they don't know, while I am willing to admit that I don't know. Although I can't tell you exactly how the Spirit of God operates, I can surely tell when He is moving in the lives and hearts of His people.

Nicodemus answered and said to Him, "How can these things be?" Jesus answered and said to him, "Are you the teacher of Israel, and do not know these things? [I can't help but believe that our Lord was giving him a very gentle rebuke here.] *Most assuredly, I say to you, We speak what We know and testify what We have seen, and you do not receive Our witness. If I have told you earthly things and you do not believe, how will you believe if I tell you heavenly things?"* (John 3:9–12 NKJV)

"Earthly things" signifies this new birth of the soul, which must take place on earth. Regeneration comes from heaven, but it is wrought on earth.

Regeneration brings about certain results. First of all, he will register a change in the life. When an individual is regenerated—that is, passes from death to life—I'm of the opinion that he will manifest something of his new Father's nature. We should be able to recognize who the Christians are, friend. Peter said:

But you are a chosen generation, a royal priesthood, a holy nation, His own special people, that you may proclaim the praises of Him who called you out of darkness [out of death] *into His marvelous light.* (1 Peter 2:9 NKJV)

If God has regenerated you, then you are a chosen generation and ought to show forth His praises. You register a change in the life, for as Paul said to the Corinthians, "If anyone is in Christ, he is a new creation" (2 Corinthians 5:17 NKJV). That doesn't mean just getting rid of a few little habits. It means that you are an entirely new, regenerated creation.

Secondly, there is a recognition of God as Father. For a child of God, it doesn't make any difference what the circumstances are—he'll always recognize that God is his Father.

> *For as many as are led by the Spirit of God, these are the sons of God. For you did not receive the spirit of bondage again to fear, but you received the Spirit of adoption by whom we cry out, "Abba, Father." The Spirit Himself bears witness with our spirit that we are children of God.* (Romans 8:14–16 NKJV)

Paul was saying that when it looks like everything is lost, when the very bottom has dropped out of life and the stars have disappeared, you can still look up as a child of God and say, "Oh, my Father, my Father." That's what the Holy Spirit does when He makes you a child of God.

Third, regeneration results in reality in prayer:

> *Likewise the Spirit also helps in our weaknesses. For we do not know what we should pray for as we ought, but the Spirit Himself makes intercession for us with groanings which cannot be uttered.* (Romans 8:26 NKJV)

God hears prayers that come from a child of His, like a little child going to his Father. And there are times, my friend, when you don't know what to ask for, but that doesn't keep you from going to Him and saying, "I don't know what to ask for, but I'd like for You to show me and direct me."

The fourth result is reality in reading the Word of God. As I've said before, I think that the greatest test for the child of God is his relationship to this book. Peter said:

> *Therefore, laying aside all malice, all deceit, hypocrisy, envy, and all evil speaking, as newborn babes, desire the pure milk of the word, that you may grow thereby, if indeed you have tasted that the Lord is gracious.* (1 Peter 2:1–3 NKJV)

If you've been born again, you are a little baby. And what do babies want? Milk. And what is the milk? The Word of God.

Have you ever seen one of those little fellas when he wants his bottle? I had an opportunity once to watch that in a hospital. I give you my word, I wish I could preach to people like that! The little ones were crying, "Boo-woo," their hands were going, their feet were going, everything was going. My, they were in motion, and it was all for that bottle. That's all they wanted. That's exactly what Peter is saying: "As newborn babes, desire the pure milk of the word." And that's an evidence you are a child of God, my friend.

Then the fifth and the last thing: there will be a regard for lost humanity. He died for the world, and if you and I are regenerated believers, we will want the world to know about Him! Not only that, but we will do something to see that the Word gets out.

And if children, then heirs—heirs of God and joint heirs
with Christ, if indeed we suffer with Him, that we may
also be glorified together. (Romans 8:17 NKJV)

You and I cannot suffer for the sins of the world as He did,
but when Paul wrote to the Colossians, he said, "[I] fill up in
my flesh what is lacking in the afflictions of Christ" (Colossians
1:24 NKJV). You and I can fill those up, if you please, by our
own desire and the things we do to get the Word out today.

What is man's responsibility to be regenerated, to become
born again?

But as many as received Him [the Lord Jesus Christ], *to*
them He gave the right [the power, the authority] *to*
become children of God, [even] *to those who* [don't do any
more nor any less than just simply] *believe in His name.*
(John 1:12 NKJV)

As someone once said, "In regeneration, man is 100 percent
passive and the Holy Spirit is 100 percent active." All He
asks you to do is to receive. A dead man can't hear or act or
see. You can't do anything to make yourself born again; the
only thing you are asked to do is receive Jesus Christ.

Not by works of righteousness which we have done, but
according to His mercy He saved us, through the washing
of regeneration and renewing of the Holy Spirit, whom
He poured out on us abundantly through Jesus Christ our
Savior. (Titus 3:5–6 NKJV)

It all rests upon Him; He saved us by the washing of regeneration and the renewing of the Holy Spirit. That's what the Spirit of God does—the moment that you and I trust Christ as Savior, He regenerates. In order to be a child of God, you must see yourself as dead in trespasses and sins, recognize that He died for you and rose again, and then go to receive everything from Him. When you do that, the Word of God guarantees that the Spirit of God will regenerate you and make you a child of God.

Chapter 8

THE HOLY SPIRIT AND INDWELLING

The indwelling ministry of the Holy Spirit is sometimes referred to as the "receiving of the Holy Spirit." That's entirely scriptural, for they both speak of the same ministry that He has in these days in which we are living. We can begin our examination of the indwelling work of the Spirit by asking the question again: where is the temple of God today?

Now, therefore, you are no longer strangers and foreigners, but fellow citizens with the saints and members of the household of God, having been built on the foundation of the apostles and prophets, Jesus Christ Himself being the chief cornerstone, in whom the whole building, being fitted together, grows into a holy temple in the Lord, in whom you also are being built together for a dwelling place of God in the Spirit. (Ephesians 2:19–22 NKJV)

Paul likened the body of believers to a temple, and this temple is the dwelling place of God today.

Now, that doesn't mean that God dwells in a building, because He does not dwell in any man-made building at all. God does dwell, however, in believers. In fact, every believer is indwelt by the Spirit of God. Paul wrote to the believers in the Corinthian church to rebuke them for being carnal, divisive, and poor saints of God. They were babes in Christ, and yet Paul wrote to them:

> *Or do you not know that your body is the temple of the Holy Spirit who is in you, whom you have from God, and you are not your own? For you were bought at a price; therefore glorify God in your body and in your spirit, which are God's.* (1 Corinthians 6:19–20 NKJV)

That's a tremendous statement. Paul didn't have much criticism of the Ephesians or the Philippians, yet he chose to say this to the carnal Corinthians: "Every one of you is indwelt by the Spirit of God." That's a great truth, by the way. And believe me, if the Corinthians were indwelt by the Spirit of God, you can write it down that the others were also. So we find here the great truth that today God does not occupy a building made with hands, but He does indwell every believer.

As a matter of fact, God has never inhabited a building. Although we touched on it earlier, I want to pause and dwell on that for a moment, because the liberals like to make this point and accuse the Old Testament church of having very crude ideas of God. I heard one liberal speaker accuse Solomon of being "primitive" because, the speaker argued, he thought God could dwell in that little temple in Jerusalem. I wish that speaker had read 2 Chronicles 6:18, because then he wouldn't have made an unfortunate statement like that. Don't get me wrong—he's a brilliant man. But apparently he had read everything else except the Bible. Notice what Solomon said at the dedication of the temple:

> *But will God indeed dwell with men on the earth?* [Here there is an implied, "Of course not!"] *Behold, heaven and the heaven of heavens cannot contain You. How much less this temple which I have built!* (2 Chronicles 6:18 NKJV)

If even the heavens and this expanding universe can't contain God, how could a little temple in Jerusalem? Solomon had a high conception of God, and he knew that God couldn't dwell in a little temple. A lot of people like to call their church "God's house," but it's not. God doesn't dwell there. When you leave, the lights are turned out, the door is locked, and there is no one in there. God doesn't dwell in a building today. But the minute the door opens and a believer walks in, God will be in that place because He indwells believers and not buildings.

Now this great truth that the Holy Spirit indwells every believer is, to my judgment, the great truth of this age in which we are living. Failure to recognize this great truth brings a spiritual stalemate. It means there can be no growth or development in a Christian's life. It also means that individual will not be able to recognize another believer. Paul said:

> *But you are not in the flesh but in the Spirit, if indeed the Spirit of God dwells in you* [that's the identifying feature]. *Now if anyone does not have the Spirit of Christ, he is not His.* (Romans 8:9 NKJV)

Since every believer is indwelt by the Holy Spirit of God, I maintain today that one can distinguish another believer. I do not mean the minute you meet him, but if you've been with an individual who's a professing Christian, you'll know in time whether he is a real believer or not. I think that the indwelling Holy Spirit makes it clear. Paul is very specific: "If anyone does not have the Spirit of Christ, he is not His." The indwelling Holy Spirit is the identifying mark of a believer.

Scripture very clearly teaches the indwelling of the Holy Spirit. I'd like to turn to just a few of the passages. At the Feast of Tabernacles, Jesus stood and cried out:

> *"If anyone thirsts, let him come to Me and drink. He who believes in Me, as the Scripture has said, out of his heart will flow rivers of living water." But this He spoke concerning the Spirit, whom those believing in Him would receive; for the Holy Spirit was not yet given, because Jesus was not yet glorified.* (John 7:37–39 NKJV)

At this point, the Spirit had not yet been given. Why? Because the Lord Jesus had not yet died. He hadn't been buried, raised from the dead, and ascended back to heaven in glory. Our Lord didn't send the Holy Spirit on His special mission until the Day of Pentecost, but this passage speaks of that day when He would come and indwell all believers.

Let's turn over a few more pages in the Gospel of John and look at another. This is the Lord Jesus speaking:

> *And I will pray the Father, and He will give you another Helper, that He may abide with you forever—the Spirit of truth, whom the world cannot receive, because it neither sees Him nor knows Him; but you know Him, for He dwells with you and will be in you.* (John 14:16–17 NKJV)

That is the indwelling of the Holy Spirit. Our Lord first said that He's been with us—I would say that's the way you'd characterize the entire Old Testament period: the Holy Spirit was in the world, with man. But the distinguishing feature of this age in which you and I live today is that now He is *in man*.

> *Now he who keeps His commandments abides* [dwells] *in Him, and He in him. And by this we know that He abides in us, by the Spirit whom He has given us.* (1 John 3:24 NKJV)

We need to recognize that the Holy Spirit is in believers and wants to have a ministry in our lives, my beloved. He wants to manifest Himself in us today.

Boy, there are too many cold clams today in the church—

people who are cold and indifferent. I want to tell you, my friend, the Holy Spirit will manifest Himself and He won't do it through pious jargon or our attendance at nice little Christian parties. Oh, my gracious, don't we have fun going to our little Christian groups—we have the best time. We're as mean as we can be outside of our group, but we sure have a good time when we're together. And there are those who think that's what makes them Christians.

My friend, I think that every one of us should examine himself and see whether he is in the faith or not. Are we indwelt by the Spirit of God? Is He manifesting Himself in our lives? And what about keeping His commandments? What is His commandment? "That you believe in Him whom He sent" (John 6:29 NKJV).

Not only that, but we also who have the firstfruits of the Spirit, even we ourselves groan within ourselves, eagerly waiting for the adoption, the redemption of our body. (Romans 8:23 NKJV)

That's a wonderful statement. Acknowledging that all the produce of the land came from God, and as an expression of thankfulness for His goodness, the Israelites would bring as an offering to Him a portion of the fruit that ripened first—and that was the Feast of Firstfruits. But it was just a precursor to the bountiful harvest that was coming. The Holy Spirit has been given to us as a firstfruit. What does that mean? It means that God has a lot more to give us. The firstfruit, the Holy Spirit, is the down payment.

And when God buys on the installment plan, He always pays it off. He's got a lot more to give us. We are to be "heirs of God and joint heirs with Christ" (Romans 8:17 NKJV).

My, what He's got in store for believers! And we need to rejoice more in the fact that we've been indwelt by the Spirit of God, who is the firstfruit of what is to come.

> *Now He who has prepared us for this very thing is God, who also has given us the Spirit as a guarantee.* (2 Corinthians 5:5 NKJV)

The King James Version reads, "given unto us the earnest of the Spirit." "Earnest money" indicates there will be more to follow. When you put down earnest money on a piece of property, it is a pledge that you are going to pay more money on that property. In such a way, God has given us the Holy Spirit, which indicates there is more to follow. This is a wonderful thing.

When people buy on the installment plan, there is a possibility that the buyer may later defect, even though he has put a down payment on the merchandise. But there is no defection in this Buyer. He has purchased us with His blood. He has put down a purchase price, which guarantees that the saved soul will be delivered safely to the Father. It means that the saved soul is in escrow today. God has put His Holy Spirit into every believer. He is the earnest. He has come into the life of the believer to bring the fullness of God to bear in our experiences.

Let's move on and notice something else. Here is a Scripture that I believe every child of God can test:

And because you are sons, God has sent forth the Spirit of His Son into your hearts [He's in there], *crying out, "Abba, Father!"* (Galatians 4:6 NKJV)

It has been my experience that the Spirit of God comes in at the time of tragedy. Have you ever been in a place where the problems have mounted up and you come to a wall and don't know where to turn? When you get to a place like that and you don't know what to do, you can go to Him and say, "My Father, my Daddy, I haven't anyplace to go. You are my Father, I'm Yours." This is the reason God lets a lot of us get down there—so we'll know we are His children. The Spirit of God, at that time, makes it real to you.

There's many a person who has had to go down through deep waters, have a broken heart, face up to something that was dark, and then cast himself upon the Father. And at that time, the Father meets him in his need. What a wonderful thing. Our Lord said:

If a son asks for bread from any father among you, will he give him a stone? Or if he asks for a fish, will he give him a serpent instead of a fish? . . . If you then, being evil, know how to give good gifts to your children, how much more will your heavenly Father give the Holy Spirit to those who ask Him! (Luke 11:11, 13 NKJV)

But you don't have to ask today. When the trials and tests come, then He ministers to you. May I say to you, friend, I believe He makes that very clear to the child of God.

Now this brings us to a rather important question in this connection: when and how does a person receive, or become indwelt by, the Holy Spirit? I say categorically and dogmatically that it is right at the moment of salvation. Paul, speaking to the "foolish Galatians," as he called them, said:

> *This only I want to learn from you: Did you receive the Spirit by the works of the law, or by the hearing of faith?* (Galatians 3:2 NKJV)

Oh, what a statement that is! He was rebuking the Galatians for trying to go back and live under the Law after having been saved by grace. Paul made it clear that they had received the Holy Spirit by faith in Christ. No other conditions were put down, my beloved.

Now notice verse 5:

> *Therefore He who supplies the Spirit to you and works miracles among you, does He do it by the works of the law, or by the hearing of faith?* (Galatians 3:5 NKJV)

Paul didn't let that one go, did he? He came back at them again, saying, "How did you get the Holy Spirit? By works? Did you do something? Did you tarry, did you wait, did you pray, did you get baptized? No! You got the Holy Spirit one way—by believing." There is no other way to receive the Holy Spirit.

Now, let's notice this principle in action.

> *Then Peter said to them, "Repent, and let every one of you be baptized in the name of Jesus Christ for the remission of sins; and you shall receive the gift of the Holy Spirit."* (Acts 2:38 NKJV)

We'll talk about baptism in a later chapter, but let's stop and deal with this just for a moment. Are you required to be baptized by water? There are some that say so. And even here Peter seemed to be giving an order: repentance, baptism by water, and then the receiving of the Holy Spirit. But remember, he was talking here to Jews on the Day of Pentecost. There was not a single Gentile there. So Peter was telling the Jews that baptism was a badge that would identify them before the other Jews. It was a step that they had to take when they came out of Judaism.

Now someone is sure to argue, "Peter said it, so this must have been the rule." Well, if it was the rule then Simon Peter forgot all about it, because when he had an opportunity to open up the Pentecost for the Gentiles, he didn't mention anything about baptism being a requirement:

> *"To Him all the prophets witness that, through His name, whosoever believes in Him will receive remission of sins." While Peter was still speaking these words, the Holy Spirit fell upon all of those who heard the word.* (Acts 10:43–44 NKJV)

The Holy Spirit came upon the Gentiles who were there in the home of Cornelius, and all Peter told them to do was believe. My friend, if baptism by water had been essential, poor Simon Peter missed the boat. But, you see, that was only for the Day of Pentecost, and it was for a very definite purpose. When Peter was there in the home of Cornelius, a Gentile, baptism was meaningless at that particular time. Baptism by water followed later.

> *And we are His witnesses to these things, and so also is the Holy Spirit whom God has given to those who obey Him.* (Acts 5:32 NKJV)

Now, what was the obedience? The way you obey Him is to "believe in Him whom He sent" (John 6:29 NKJV). That's exactly what Peter said to Simon Magus:

> *But Peter said to him, "Your money perish with you, because you thought that the gift of God could be purchased with money!"* (Acts 8:20 NKJV)

That gift of God was the Holy Spirit, and the very fact He was called "a gift" is interesting. The Holy Spirit again and again in the Book of Acts and in the Epistles is spoken of as a gift that is given to believers. How do you receive a gift? Do you wait for it? Do you ask for it? Do you pay for it? Do you promise something for it? Or do you just believe and hold out your hand and somebody gives it to you? That's the only way in the world you can receive a gift.

A man once told me at a Bible class that he had something for me in his car. He didn't say anything about paying for it, he didn't say anything about selling it, he said, "I've got something for you, a gift." He brought me the loveliest basket of the most luscious fruit you've ever seen, and, you know, to this day I haven't paid that fellow. I just thanked him. I didn't have to tarry for it; I didn't have to wait for it; I didn't have to ask for it.

I think one of the silliest things for believers to do today is ask, "Lord, give me the Holy Spirit." Thank the Lord He has a sense of humor! I think sometimes He'd like to reach out and say, "I've already given Him to you. Don't ask Me for what you've already got. If you're My child, you've already received the Holy Spirit." We need to believe God, you see.

I want to notice several of the objections to the truth that the Holy Spirit indwells every believer at the moment of salvation. There are those who say, "No, you can't receive the Spirit by faith alone. You must tarry, you must pray to receive the Holy Spirit, you must have somebody lay hands on you." Now, it's all right to disagree with me as long as you'll just listen to what the Word of God has to say. So let's look at several of these arguments.

I know we've gone over this before, but it's important and warrants repeating. Before Pentecost, our Lord said, "Tarry in the city of Jerusalem until you are endued with power from on high" (Luke 24:49 NKJV). At that point, the Day of Pentecost had yet to take place. They were to wait until that day came. But we today are on the other side of it; we no longer wait for it. We don't go back to Pentecost because we are already past it.

Someone, actually a friend of mine, wrote an article in which he said, "What we need to do is get back to Pentecost." That's the problem today—there are too many trying to get back there! We are not told to go back to that day. Those men were to wait in Jerusalem until the experience of the Holy Spirit coming on the Day of Pentecost. They had to tarry, but you and I do not have to tarry.

Then there is the most interesting and unusual case of Simon Magus and the Samaritans. Philip preached the gospel in Samaria, and many men and women believed (see Acts 8:12). Simon came in contact with Philip, and apparently he made a profession of faith under the ministry of Philip. I believe that Simon was the first religious racketeer in the church—but, unfortunately, not the last. He professed to be a believer during the sweeping revival in Samaria under the ministry of Philip. So Simon believed, and was baptized and became a friend of Philip.

You would certainly think that he was a real child of God. However, he was not converted. There are also others who are professing believers, but they are not born again. They have the head knowledge, they go along with the crowd, but they are not saved. Although they have been baptized with water, they have not been baptized into the church of Jesus Christ by the Holy Spirit.

There are a great many people like that today. I receive many letters from people who have told me that since they have been studying the Bible along with our program, they have begun to examine their faith. Many have come to realize that they have just been following along with someone else and that they have not been genuinely, personally converted. Paul said, "Examine yourselves as to whether you are in the faith. Test yourselves" (2 Corinthians 13:5 NKJV). It is a very good thing to check yourself. See whether you are in the faith or not.

The man Simon had all the outward trappings. He answered that he did believe in Jesus, and so he was baptized. But it was not a genuine faith.

> *Now when the apostles who were at Jerusalem heard that Samaria had received the word of God, they sent Peter and John to them, who, when they had come down, prayed for them that they might receive the Holy Spirit. For as yet He had fallen upon none of them. They had only been baptized in the name of the Lord Jesus.* (Acts 8:14–16 NKJV)

When the apostles heard that there was a great moving of the Spirit down in Samaria, they sent Peter and John to check on it. They found a great company of professing believers who had not been born again. They had not been baptized into the church by the Holy Spirit. They were not indwelt by the Spirit of God. They had gone through an outward ceremony, but they were not saved. My friend, being baptized with water or going through some other ceremony will not make you a Christian.

Then this is, to my judgment, the most interesting case of all. I love this one because people like to confront me with this passage and say, "Look at this. These people in Ephesus believed, and they did not receive the Holy Spirit." All right, let's look at it:

> *And it happened while Apollos was at Corinth, that Paul, having passed through the upper regions, came to Ephesus. And finding some disciples he said to them, "Did you receive the Holy Spirit when you believed?"* (Acts 19:1–2 NKJV)

Paul was saying, "Why didn't you receive the Holy Spirit the moment you believed? There is something wrong here."

You may recall that Apollos did not know anything about the death and resurrection of Jesus Christ until Aquila and Priscilla talked to him (see Acts 18:26). All he had been preaching was the baptism of John, which was as far as his knowledge went. As a result of this, the people who had heard his preaching had been instructed only as far as the baptism of John and had not even heard of the Holy Spirit. Paul detected that they had not been taught about the Lord Jesus and didn't know anything about Pentecost.

> *And he said to them, "Into what then were you baptized?" So they said, "Into John's baptism."* (Acts 19:3 NKJV)

You see, these people were baptized, but they were not saved. And they had not received the Holy Spirit because they were not saved.

Friend, the moment you trust Christ you are regenerated

by the Holy Spirit, you are indwelt by the Spirit of God, you are sealed by the Spirit of God, and you are baptized into the body of believers by the Spirit of God. This happens the moment you believe and trust Christ.

The Ephesians were wonderful people, but they were not saved, my beloved. The evidence was that they were not indwelt by the Spirit of God. But notice this:

> *Then Paul said, "John indeed baptized with a baptism of repentance, saying to the people that they should believe on Him who would come after him, that is, on Christ Jesus." When they heard this, they were baptized in the name of the Lord Jesus. And when Paul had laid hands on them, the Holy Spirit came upon them, and they spoke with tongues and prophesied.* (Acts 19:4–6 NKJV)

May I say, we have here one of the most remarkable incidents in Scripture. Then these other things took place (their speaking in tongues, their being baptized), but my friend, none of these things had anything in the world to do with being indwelt by the Spirit of God. Under the circumstances, there was evidence needed to prove the Ephesians had truly been filled with the Spirit. The evidence in this case was that they were given the gift of tongues. People today try to argue that speaking in tongues is proof that you have been baptized by the Holy Spirit or been indwelt by the Spirit of God. But this is not a rule—it was evidence, in this specific case, of their indwelling.

Allow me to illustrate an important point by turning to Paul's conversion:

> *And Ananias went his way and entered the house; and laying his hands on him he said, "Brother Saul, the Lord Jesus, who appeared to you on the road as you came, has sent me that you may receive your sight and be filled with the Holy Spirit." Immediately there fell from his eyes something like scales, and he received his sight at once; and he arose and was baptized.* (Acts 9:17–18 NKJV)

Do you have to be baptized in order to be indwelt? Paul the Apostle was saved, regenerated, indwelt, and filled by the Holy Spirit before he was ever baptized. I say to you, you cannot make a rule from just one instance.

Have you received the Holy Spirit? Do you have the assurance of His presence in your life? Honestly, I think a lot of Christians today ought to ask themselves, "Am I just bluffing my way along, just trying to keep up appearances? Do I pose as a Christian by using pious platitudes and a holy attitude? Am I real or am I a phony?" Why don't you settle it once and for all?

My friend, I think a great many of us need to get on our knees and pray, "Oh, God, I receive the Holy Spirit, and I want tangible evidence in my life that I'm Your child, indwelt by Your Spirit." We need that today above everything else.

Chapter 9

THE BAPTIZING MINISTRY OF THE HOLY SPIRIT

The baptizing work of the Holy Spirit is probably the most controversial of any of the ministries of the Holy Spirit. This is due largely to a misunderstanding of what the baptism of the Holy Spirit truly means. It is the peculiar and, I would say, unique ministry of this age in which we are living today. The baptism of the Holy Spirit did not begin until the Day of Pentecost, and it will be discontinued when the church is removed from this earthly scene at the Rapture.

Probably the most lucid and succinct statement that we have on the baptizing ministry of the Holy Spirit is:

For as the body is one and has many members, but all the members of that one body, being many, are one body, so also is Christ. For by one Spirit we were all baptized into one body—whether Jews or Greeks, whether slaves or free—and

> *have all been made to drink into one Spirit. For in fact the*
> *body is not one member but many.* (1 Corinthians 12:12–14
> NKJV)

The baptizing work of the Holy Spirit is what makes us members of this one body, called the church or the body of Christ.

Now the word "baptize" is an often misunderstood word. The root, *bapto*, means "to dip" and is found in three places in the New Testament. You may recall the story our Lord gave of the poor beggar, Lazarus, and the rich man—both of whom died. The rich man called out from the place of torment, "Send Lazarus that he may dip [*bapto*] the tip of his finger in water and cool my tongue" (Luke 16:24 NKJV). Then in John 13:26 (NKJV), the Lord Jesus said, "It is he to whom I shall give a piece of bread when I have dipped [*bapto*] it." And, finally, the most striking usage of all appears in the Book of Revelation when John spoke of the rider on the white horse: "He was clothed with a robe dipped [*bapto*] in blood, and His name is called The Word of God" (Revelation 19:13 NKJV).

The word "baptize" that we use, and which is used in 1 Corinthians 12, is the Greek *baptizo*. This word means to physically envelop in an element, to come under the influence, or to identify with. In other words, that which comes under the influence of something becomes identified with it. For example, the teacher has influence over a pupil until, finally, the pupil thinks like the teacher, speaks like the teacher, espouses what the teacher says, and, therefore, becomes identified (or baptized) with the teacher.

When the translators came to this word, *baptizo*, they did not translate it into an English word. Instead, they transliterated it; that is, they just spelled it out in our alphabet and made it into "baptize." So these folk today who are so dogmatic about what "baptize" means might be interested to know that it is not an English word at all, and if they would look it up in a Greek lexicon they'd find several different meanings for the word *baptizo*. But primarily, it means to envelop physically or put something in an element.

To illustrate, suppose a housewife has a piece of white cloth that has turned a little gray or dirty, and now she wants to make it blue. She gets some blue dye, takes that cloth, and dips it in (puts it down into, envelops it in) that dye. The cloth is overwhelmed by it, and so it comes out blue. It's been baptized, and that's the word as it is used in the Greek. If you can grab hold of that meaning, it will help you a great deal as we begin to look deeper into this issue of baptism.

REAL BAPTISM

Now, as far as the Word of God is concerned, there is real baptism and there is ritual (or water) baptism. Real baptism is by the Holy Spirit: "For by one Spirit we were all baptized into one body" (1 Corinthians 12:13 NKJV). That is to say, the Spirit of God takes us, envelops us, makes us a member of that body, and we now are put in the body of Christ and identified with Him. That's the meaning of real baptism.

I hate to see this wonderful, precious word abused today.

It has even been taken and made into a form of fanaticism that teaches we must go and seek the baptism of the Holy Spirit— even though every believer is told that he has already been baptized by the Spirit of God! We don't have to seek for that which we already have; every believer has already been put in the body of Christ by the baptizing work of the Holy Spirit.

It's like the dear little Scotch lady who believed she was safe as a believer. Someone questioned her, "You think you are safe?" She replied, "Oh, yes. My Shepherd says that nothing can pluck me out of His hand." The first party asked, "But suppose you slip down through His fingers?" The dear lady responded, "That couldn't be—I am one of His fingers." May I say to you, that's the meaning of "baptize." Being put in the body of Christ makes us one and identifies us with Him. What a glorious meaning it has! *That's* real baptism.

BAPTISM BY WATER AND FIRE

I believe that ritual baptism, meaning a physical baptism by water, sets forth the work of the Holy Spirit. It's an outward sign of an inward work. It is mentioned in the Word of God; in fact, the Bible has a great deal to say about ritual baptism. One such instance is recorded in the Gospel of Matthew when John the Baptist said:

> *I indeed baptize you with water unto repentance, but He who is coming after me is mightier than I, whose sandals*

I am not worthy to carry. He will baptize you with the Holy Spirit and fire. (Matthew 3:11 NKJV)

Notice that John said he baptized with water—that's ritual. But the baptism by fire that he mentioned is not for today. The baptism of fire comes in the Great Tribulation period— it's judgment. This is the day of the baptism of the Holy Spirit, and the baptism of fire won't come until after the church is removed and judgment comes upon the earth. You see, there have already been two thousand years in that little "and" connecting "He will baptize you with the Holy Spirit" and "fire."

TWOFOLD APPLICATION

That brings us to another point about the word "baptism": it has a twofold meaning in the way it is to be applied. First, it is prophecy, with Christ as the baptizing agent and the Holy Spirit as the influence; then it is fulfillment, with the Holy Spirit as the baptizing agent and Christ (or the church) as the element.

Notice another Scripture that speaks prophetically of Christ baptizing believers with the Holy Spirit:

John answered, saying to all, "I indeed baptize you with water; but One mightier than I is coming, whose sandal strap I am not worthy to loose. He will baptize you with the Holy Spirit and fire." (Luke 3:16 NKJV)

But, as I said, fire is not for today.

> *I did not know Him, but He who sent me to baptize with water said to me, "Upon whom you see the Spirit descending, and remaining on Him, this is He who baptizes with the Holy Spirit." And I have seen and testified that this is the Son of God.* (John 1:33–34 NKJV)

These Scriptures are prophetic—they speak of the fact that when He came, He would baptize. So this is the age in which we have the peculiar baptizing ministry of the Holy Spirit, and the baptism of fire is yet future.

But when we come to the fulfillment, other Scriptures present the Holy Spirit as the baptizing agent and Christ as the element of the church of the body of Christ. We've already looked at one such passage, 1 Corinthians 12:12–13. Of course there are many others, and we'll turn to them in another connection later. They all speak of Christ as the head of the body and the fact that believers are, today, in Christ.

FILLING VERSUS BAPTISM

How did we get in Christ? Through the baptizing work of the Holy Spirit—that's what baptism means. When you trusted Christ as Savior, the Holy Spirit not only regenerated, indwelt, and sealed you, but He also baptized you, which means He put you in the body of Christ. So you are now identified in Christ, my beloved.

This is illustrated in one of the greatest verses that we have in the Word of God (I *know* it is the most difficult verse), which is John 14:20 (NKJV). The Lord Jesus was speaking in the Upper Room:

> *At that day* [the Day of Pentecost] *you will know that I am in My Father, and you in Me, and I in you.*

When the Day of Pentecost came, it was "you in Me, and I in you." Seven monosyllabic words: four pronouns, two prepositions, and one conjunction. They're just little bitty one-cylinder words. You can take any one of those words and a child could tell you what it means, but there is not a theologian living or who ever has lived who can tell you what these seven words mean when put together like this. This is the most profound statement in the Word of God.

"You in Me"—that is salvation, the baptizing work of the Holy Spirit to put the believer in Christ. "And I in you"—that's sanctification, the filling of the Holy Spirit. Sanctification is where work begins, service begins, and fruit begins. Water baptism hasn't anything to do with it, by the way, because the filling of the Holy Spirit is an experience and baptism of the Holy Spirit is not.

Exposing the Myths

You may remember that our Lord said: "For John truly baptized with water, but you shall be baptized with the Holy

Spirit not many days from now" (Acts 1:5 NKJV). But on the Day of Pentecost, does Scripture say, "And they were all baptized with the Holy Spirit"? No! It says they were all "filled" with the Holy Spirit (see Acts 2:4). Why? Because these men were going to be speaking in other tongues (not *un*known tongues; they were going to speak in known languages), and they were going to serve. And in order for them to serve, they needed the experience of the filling of the Spirit.

The baptism of the Holy Spirit is never related to experience. Someone may wonder, "Weren't they baptized, too?" Of course they were, but the point is they were going to serve, and in order to serve they had to be filled. The baptism of the Holy Spirit hasn't anything to do with service or experience. The filling is the experience, and it is for service.

If you read some older commentaries, you might notice that the writers sometimes use the word "baptize" to mean "filling." But that was back in the days when you did not have to be as sharp with terms, because there were not these groups as we have today that go off on tangents trying to make the word "baptize" mean something it doesn't. That's how the whole business of "seeking the baptism of the Holy Spirit" got started.

And among those who teach that we ought to be seeking out baptism, many misrepresent the rest of us by suggesting that we don't believe baptism is necessary at all! I believe that the baptism of the Holy Spirit is essential. In fact, you're not a believer unless you've been baptized by the Holy Spirit. But I do not believe it is an *experience*. Every believer has been baptized by the Spirit of God. Those on the fanatical fringe ought not to misrepresent us by saying we do not believe in the baptism; we just don't believe that it is an experience.

These same people have been known to teach that we are to wait for the Holy Spirit. May I say how false it is to tell people they are to tarry for the Holy Spirit? Where did our Lord tell us to tarry? He told his apostles to wait for the Day of Pentecost, but no one today is to wait for the Day of Pentecost—it's already come! It's a matter of history, and the Spirit of God is here today. The minute any individual puts his faith in Jesus Christ, he's regenerated, indwelt, and baptized by the Spirit of God.

In Christ

Now I want to go back to 1 Corinthians 12, because this section of Scripture is basic to an understanding of the Holy Spirit today.

> *For as the body is one and has many members, but all the members of that one body, being many, are one body, so also is Christ.* (1 Corinthians 12:12 NKJV)

Paul called the church (that is, the body of believers) "Christ." So what he was actually saying here was: "So also is Christ [one body], but this one body has many members." How can I, a sinner, get into the body of Christ? By being baptized by the Holy Spirit! "For by one Spirit we were all baptized into one body" (1 Corinthians 12:13 NKJV). He didn't tell the Corinthians they were to tarry for it. He didn't tell them it was something reserved only for special people. The very interesting thing is that he told them they were already baptized by the Holy Spirit.

Now, remember, who were the Corinthians? They were the most worldly church of all. Paul started out by telling them: "There are divisions among you. You are carnal; you are not spiritual—you're babes in Christ." (See 1 Corinthians 3:1–3.) But at the same time, he said to them here in 1 Corinthians 12 that they had been baptized by the Holy Spirit because they'd trusted Christ.

It was not by accident that God chose the carnal Corinthians to receive this message from Paul. You see, this baptism is not an experience, and it's not intended to create supersaints. Its purpose is to put you in the body of Christ, my beloved—that's the baptism.

> *For as many of you as were baptized into Christ have put on Christ.* (Galatians 3:27 NKJV)

You have been baptized, and you have put on Christ. The impression is that these two things happen simultaneously. But the Greek won't allow us to give it that exact meaning. Let me give you the literal translation of this: in the act of being baptized, you put on Christ. The two actions are identical. Being baptized by the Spirit of God and putting on Christ (*becoming* Christ, part of the body of Christ) are the same thing. This is one of the greatest truths that we have today!

Do you understand now why I'm contending that this thing not be reduced to some little sentimental experience that may lead to fanaticism? I have become a member of the body of Christ, and I became a member by the baptism of the Holy Spirit.

There is a passage of Scripture that, to me, clarifies this above everything else:

> **What shall we say then?** [Paul was talking to Roman believers. He'd gone over salvation with them, and next he was going to talk to them about living the Christian life.] **Shall we continue in sin that grace may abound?** (Romans 6:1 NKJV)

In other words, just because you're saved by grace, does that mean you can continue in sin? The next verse reveals God's answer: "Certainly not!" (Romans 6:2 NKJV). If you think you can go on living in sin, you're not a child of God. If you buy into this idea today that you can be as mean as you want to be simply because you're a member of a certain church, you're not a Christian.

Some may want to argue with me on that point and say, "You can't say I'm not a Christian, because I'm saved by grace." If you've been saved by grace, shall you continue in sin? Your answer must be, "Certainly not! I hate it, and I am not going to be mean, I am not going to undermine other believers or talk behind their backs, and I'll not do these dirty things that believers are doing today." If you're a child of God, you won't do those things. You're a member of His body, that other believer is a member of His body, and you wouldn't hurt another of your own body, would you?

Certainly not! How shall we who died to sin live any longer in it? (Romans 6:2 NKJV)

Let me take a moment to clarify this. We are not dead to sin. I haven't met a single saint who is dead to sin. However, we have died to sin. When did we die to sin? More than two thousand years ago when Christ died to sin for us, we died in Him. How do I know that? Notice what comes next:

Or do you not know that as many of us as were baptized into Christ Jesus were baptized into His death? (Romans 6:3 NKJV)

What happened? Well, we were identified with Christ. How were we identified with Him? We were baptized into (identified into) His death. So when Christ died for us, our sins died with Him.

Your sins today are in one of two places: they are either on you waiting for judgment, or they were left back yonder with Christ when He died on the cross. Where are your sins today? There is no third place for them. For that's the meaning:

Therefore we were buried with Him through baptism [by identification] *into death, that just as Christ was raised from the dead by the glory of the Father, even so we also should walk in newness of life.* (Romans 6:4 NKJV)

When Christ died, we died. When He was raised from the dead, we were raised from the dead. We are *in* Christ, seated in the heavenlies with Him. How did we get there? By the baptism of the Holy Spirit who identified us with Christ, buried our sins with Him by identification, and raised us up with Him.

> *Buried with Him in baptism, in which you also were raised with Him through faith in the working of God, who raised Him from the dead.* (Colossians 2:12 NKJV)

UNITY OF THE SPIRIT

By the baptism of the Holy Spirit, we've all been put in one body, and that body is Christ. Now, what are we to do? We are to keep the unity of the Spirit.

> *Endeavoring to keep the unity of the Spirit in the bond of peace.* (Ephesians 4:3 NKJV)

We are not told to *make* the unity of the Spirit; the unity was already made when we entered the body of Christ through baptism.

> *There is one body* [the body of believers] *and one* [Holy] *Spirit, just as you were called in one hope of your calling; one Lord* [the Lord Jesus Christ], *one faith* [saving faith in Him], *one baptism* [What baptism? Baptism of the

Holy Spirit. Don't tell me this is referring to water baptism; there's not a drop of water here. It is the baptism of the Holy Spirit that put you in the body of believers, my beloved.]*; one God and Father of all, who is above all, and through all, and in you all.* (Ephesians 4:4–6 NKJV)

This is a wonderful thing! Some like to say that "one baptism" refers to a mode of water baptism or is a reference back to Pentecost. But it is not. It is the baptism of the Holy Spirit, if you please.

I had two uncles who were preachers in the Church of Christ. One of them once said to me, "Vernon, you have to be baptized to be saved." I said, "You know, you and I agree on that. Let's shake hands." He answered back, "What do you mean? Have you changed your mind on that issue?" I said, "No, you just stated a great truth: we need to be baptized to be saved. The only difference is that you think it's with water, and I think it's the baptism of the Holy Spirit." We have to be put in the body of believers, and the Spirit of God is the one who does that through His baptism.

ILLUSTRATION OF MOSES

By way of illustration, let's turn to the writer to the Hebrews for the interpretation of the Spirit concerning this:

Moreover, brethren, I do not want you to be unaware that all our fathers were under the cloud, all passed through

the sea [the Red Sea], all were baptized into Moses in the
cloud and in the sea. (1 Corinthians 10:1–2 NKJV)

They were all baptized into Moses. Are you going to try to tell me that was water baptism? I hope not. The real meaning of the word is that they were *identified* into Moses. They came under the influence of Moses, the leader, and were identified with him.

That is the way the account is given back in Exodus (see Exodus 13:17–14:31). The Israelites came to the Red Sea, and I imagine that night the wind was blowing and the waves were coming in and breaking on the shore. In back of them, they saw the chariots of the Egyptians approaching through the dust of the desert. Those poor people said to Moses, "Why in the world did you bring us out here to the desert to die? Weren't there enough graves in Egypt? We don't want to die here! Let's go back to the brickyards of Egypt—they weren't nearly as bad as we thought they were."

What did Moses do? He went down and stretched his hand over the sea. All that night, it rolled back as the people whined, murmured, and complained. You see, they had no faith and wanted to turn back. Yet in the morning, "By faith they passed through the Red Sea as by dry land, whereas the Egyptians, attempting to do so, were drowned" (Hebrews 11:29 NKJV). By whose faith did they pass through? Was it their faith? No, they had none. It was *Moses'* faith.

When Moses started walking out across the dried seabed, they followed him. The Book of Exodus tells us that when they reached the other shore, they sang the song of

Moses. They had been brought under his influence and were thereby baptized into Moses. They were redeemed and delivered, but it was by the faith of Moses, so they were then identified with him.

Another One went through the dark waters of death for me. And, by faith, I take His hand and go through. Buried with Him by identification, I come out on the other side raised to newness of life, my beloved. This hasn't anything in the world to do with water at all, because who really got wet? The Egyptians who attempted to cross got soaked! They really got water baptized. I do not think the children of Israel even got damp. But they were baptized into Moses, just as we are baptized into the body of Christ.

"In"

Theologians have looked all over for one word that would describe this work of redemption, but they've never found it. They have come up with "propitiation," "reconciliation," "redemption," and "salvation," but not one of these words gives a full-orbed picture and covers the entire spectrum of salvation. But God has given one word, and that one word is the little preposition "in."

We are *in* Christ through baptism of the Holy Spirit. There are only two classes of people in the world: those that are in Christ and those that are out of Christ. Those that are in Christ are completely and perfectly saved, because they trusted Him. Those that are out of Christ are absolutely lost. There's no middle ground. You're either in Christ by the baptism of the Holy Spirit, or you're out of Christ.

I have come to several conclusions. One is that all believers are baptized—not some believers, but *all* believers. Remember that even the carnal Corinthians were "all baptized into one body . . . into one Spirit" (1 Corinthians 12:13 NKJV). And if all the sinful Corinthians were baptized, you may be sure that all believers today are as well.

The second conclusion I'd like to point out is that this baptism takes place at the very moment of salvation. Take note of this particular passage of Scripture:

> *While Peter was still speaking these words, the Holy Spirit fell upon all those who heard the word. And those of the circumcision who believed were astonished, as many as came with Peter, because the gift of the Holy Spirit had been poured out on the Gentiles also. For they heard them speak with tongues and magnify God. Then Peter answered, "Can anyone forbid water, that these should not be baptized who have received the Holy Spirit just as we have?" And he commanded them to be baptized in the name of the Lord.* (Acts 10:44–48 NKJV)

This was the Gentile Pentecost, by the way. You'll notice there was no mention of tarrying for the Holy Spirit, and it was not an experience they needed to seek out (those are my third and fourth conclusions, by the way). They believed, and immediately the Holy Spirit was upon them.

Let's turn to one more passage that illustrates this. When Paul went to Ephesus, as we've seen, he said to the believers there, "Did you receive the Holy Spirit when you believed?" (Acts 19:2 NKJV). He did not say "since you believed" or "after you believed." It is "*when* you believed." At the very moment when you believed, you received His Spirit and were also baptized by the Spirit of God. It's important to note here again that this baptism is not an experience. The *filling* on the Day of Pentecost was an experience for those who were present. But because the Holy Spirit has united believers in the body of Christ, it is not an experience for us.

My fifth point is that the baptism of the Holy Spirit is not for power. After all, these Corinthians had no power because they were carnal believers. Paul said he couldn't even write to them "as to spiritual people but as to carnal" (1 Corinthians 3:1 NKJV). He had to speak to the Galatians pretty plainly as well. You may recall that he rebuked them sternly (see Galatians 3:1 and 5:4). And yet he was also able to say to them, "For as many of you as were baptized into Christ have put on Christ" (Galatians 3:27 NKJV). By being baptized, they had put on Christ. Just like the Galatians, we are powerless to live the Christian life unless we put on the power of Christ.

Sixth, baptism is not a sign of superspirituality. Again, witness the Corinthians and the Galatians—would anyone categorize them as super-duper saints? No! And yet even they were securely in Christ.

The seventh conclusion is that it creates unity among believers. Remember this:

> *Endeavoring to keep the unity of the Spirit in the bond of peace . . . One God and Father of all, who is above all, and through all, and in you all.* (Ephesians 4:3, 6 NKJV)

The baptism of the Holy Spirit creates unity, and we are told to keep the unity of the Spirit. Isn't it strange that the issue of believers being united through the baptism of the Holy Spirit has actually divided God's people? That ought not to be. Christians should not be divided.

That unity among believers means also that we are one with Christ forever, which is my eighth point. We're not put in Christ temporarily. This is the case regardless of your mode of water baptism. Water baptism cannot even illustrate baptism of the Holy Spirit because anything that you put down into water, or put water on, has to come out of the water eventually. But when we are baptized into Christ, we are there to stay! We're not put in and taken out, because when we are baptized into Christ, we become part of His body.

The ninth and final point is that we are never commanded to be baptized with the Holy Spirit. Nowhere in all of these references that I've given you is a believer commanded to be baptized by the Holy Spirit. Isn't that interesting? There are those today who say that we need to seek the baptism, to *do* something to gain it. Well, where's my command for that?

Where am I commanded to be baptized? The baptism of the Holy Spirit is not a command given to us, nor is it an experience. It is an act of God whereby the believer in Jesus Christ is indwelt by the Spirit of God, sealed unto the day of redemption, and placed into the church—the body of Christ.

Chapter 10

THE FILLING OF
THE SPIRIT

As we have just seen, nowhere in the world are believers commanded to be baptized, but the Christian *is* commanded to be filled with the Spirit:

> **And do not be drunk with wine, in which is dissipation; but be filled with the Spirit.** (Ephesians 5:18 NKJV)

For a person to be filled, the Holy Spirit must occupy every area of the believer's life. The figure used is like a glass filled with water, and it's a marvelous illustration. You could fill a glass with marbles, but they wouldn't fill every area. But when Paul spoke of being filled with the Holy Spirit, it was like a liquid. Liquid goes into every crevice of the life, and the Christian who is filled with the Spirit of God is one in whom the Spirit of God occupies all of his life—not just on Sundays or in just one area of his life, but in his *entire* life.

A great many people say, "If only I could get more of the Holy Spirit." But that's never the question; the question is, can the Holy Spirit get more of you? He wants to occupy believers completely, and that's what being filled means.

Why are we to be filled with the Holy Spirit? What is the purpose? Let's notice two passages of Scripture:

> *Behold, I send the Promise of My Father upon you; but tarry in the city of Jerusalem until you are endued with power from on high.* (Luke 24:49 NKJV)

> *But you shall receive power when the Holy Spirit has come upon you; and you shall be witnesses to Me in Jerusalem, and in all Judea and Samaria, and to the end of the earth.* (Acts 1:8 NKJV)

Now, I must call your attention to something important: Does it say, "You shall receive power after the Holy Spirit baptizes you?" No. Never is baptism associated with power. Power comes with being filled.

As we saw in Ephesians 5:18, there is a figure of speech used in Scripture that compares being filled with the Spirit to being filled with wine. That same comparison is made in two other places. Concerning John the Baptist, the angel said to Zacharias:

> *For he will be great in the sight of the Lord, and shall drink neither wine nor strong drink. He will also be*

filled with the Holy Spirit, even from his mother's womb.
(Luke 1:15 NKJV)

Two things are said here: he'll not drink wine or strong drink, but he will be filled with the Holy Spirit.

The last reference is in Luke's record of the Day of Pentecost. Those present were filled with the Holy Spirit and began witnessing, not in an unknown tongue, but every one in a tongue he understood:

So they were all amazed and perplexed, saying to one another, "Whatever could this mean?" Others mocking said, "They are full of new wine." (Acts 2:12–13 NKJV)

I'm going to say something that may seem a little strange. Tonight, every bar in every city will be filled with people crawling up on bar stools and asking for cocktails or drinks of some sort. Why do they do it? There are many reasons, of course. But by and large, the main reason that most of them start is because they are compensating for a great need or lack in their own life.

I have a friend, he and I grew up together, and he became a drunkard. He visited me once, and we got down and prayed until he cried like a baby. He didn't give up drinking at that time, but later he did. He kept crying out to God, and God gave him a wonderful deliverance. But when he was still a drunkard, I asked him, "Why in the world do you keep drinking this stuff—do you love it like that?" He said, "No, I hate it." So I asked him how he managed to get hooked on it if he hated it so much. He answered me, "Well, in a group I was always an introvert. I never could express myself. Then I went out with some fellas, and I had a couple of cans of beer, and, boy, I was patting everybody on the back and all of a sudden I was sociable. That's when I started."

You see, the drink was meeting a need that was inside of him—it was compensation for something. I'm not trying to offer an excuse, but how many lonesome people tonight will crawl up on a bar stool? They don't want to face whatever it is they are lacking. I once had a letter from a lady who wrote, "I can't stand to face that empty room another day." You see, there are a lot of folk today who have a great need, something lacking. Paul said to believers, "Do not be drunk with wine, in which is dissipation" (Ephesians 5:18 NKJV); you'll become an alcoholic if you go that route. But the Spirit of God can make up that need and bring joy.

When bystanders at the Day of Pentecost saw those men of God filled with the Spirit and then heard them start talking in other languages, some believed, but others said, "Boy, are they drunk!" Have you ever heard a drunk fella laugh for no reason in the world? (You ought to see him the next day—he's not laughing then; but that night, boy, does he laugh.) No one would ever suspect us of being drunk today, would they? Oh, how we need today a filling of the Holy Spirit—it brings joy to the life.

I want to call attention to some people in the pages of Scripture who were filled by the Holy Spirit. We've already seen where the angel predicted that John the Baptist would be filled with the Holy Spirit, and of course there were those who witnessed on the Day of Pentecost. But you may also recall that when Mary went to visit her cousin, the child leaped in Elizabeth's womb and she was filled with the Spirit (see Luke 1:41). When Zacharias gave a prophecy concerning his son, John the Baptist, Scripture prefaces it by saying that Zacharias was also filled with the Holy Spirit (see Luke 1:67). Even the Lord Jesus Himself, after His testing, needed the strengthening of the Spirit of God (see Luke 4:14).

And if He needed the power of the Spirit of God, then you and I *certainly* need it! And I would have you note that throughout the entire Book of Acts, no service was ever performed for God that was not done by Spirit-filled men and women. That explains a whole lot today. That explains why Sunday school classes peter out. That explains why an individual who wants to serve and goes at it his own way, makes such a miserable failure of it. Why? Because he's not being filled by the Spirit of God, my beloved. You and I cannot do anything for God in our own strength or energy. We must be filled by the Spirit of God.

The first major persecution of the church is recorded in the Book of Acts. To my judgment, that church coming together in prayer was one of the most wonderful things recorded in Scripture. But if I had joined that prayer meeting, do you know what I would have prayed for? I'd have said, "Oh, Lord, stop this persecution—I don't like it." But listen to how the early church members prayed in their time of persecution:

"Now, Lord, look on their threats, and grant to Your servants that with all boldness they may speak Your word [they didn't ask for the persecution to stop; they just asked for courage to speak out the Word], *by stretching out Your hand to heal, and that signs and wonders may be done through the name of Your holy Servant Jesus." And when they had prayed, the place where they were assembled together was shaken; and they were all filled with the Holy Spirit and they spoke the word of God with boldness.* (Acts 4:29–31 NKJV)

Speaking the Word of God in boldness, my beloved, comes from being filled with the Spirit. In the times of persecution, the early church grew as it's never grown since then. Persecution has never hurt the church, but lukewarmness is killing the church today. We need to be more like the early church—those men and women were filled with the Spirit:

Therefore, brethren, seek out from among you seven men of good reputation, full of the Holy Spirit and wisdom, whom we may appoint over this business. (Acts 6:3 NKJV)

When the nominating committee was picking officers for the early church, whom did they pick? Did they say, "Well, this one's a good fellow. He has a good personality. And this man is a good businessman . . ."? No. They wanted men who were filled with the Holy Spirit. What we need more than anything else today, are Spirit-filled leaders capable of carrying on the business of the church, my beloved.

Whom did the early church choose? Stephen, "a man of faith and the Holy Spirit" (Acts 6:5 NKJV). Stephen was also the first martyr of the church. That's the caliber of man chosen by the early church to lead. Notice what Scripture says about Stephen's stoning:

But he, being full of the Holy Spirit, gazed into heaven and saw the glory of God, and Jesus standing at the right hand of God. (Acts 7:55 NKJV)

Paul was in attendance as that Spirit-filled man of God was martyred. We read later of Paul's own conversion:

And Ananias went his way and entered the house; and laying his hands on him he said, "Brother Saul, the Lord Jesus, who appeared to you on the road as you came, has sent me that you may receive your sight and be filled with the Holy Spirit." (Acts 9:17 NKJV)

Now, here was the most brilliant man who ever walked this earth (I think he had the highest IQ of any man), and yet God said, "I can't use him until he's filled with the Spirit of God."

What do we need today? Do we need to seek the baptism? Oh, no, the child of God has already been baptized. But, my, how you and I need the filling of the Spirit of God!

Chapter 11

GRIEVING THE
SPIRIT

We have already seen the importance of being filled with the Holy Spirit. In fact, it is a requirement if we are to be of service, have power, and live the Christian life today. But there is one thing that, probably more than anything else, keeps us from being filled: sin in the believer's life. Sin not only prevents us from being filled, but it actually grieves the Holy Spirit:

> *And do not grieve the Holy Spirit of God, by whom you were sealed for the day of redemption.* (Ephesians 4:30 NKJV)

There are several basic truths to be learned from this verse that we ought to establish at the very beginning. First, as we've already seen, the Holy Spirit is a person. You cannot grieve an influence; you can only grieve a person. Second, you cannot grieve Him away. We are told very clearly here that we are sealed by the Holy Spirit "for the day of redemption." I have my own very interesting translation I'd like to share: "And do not grieve the Holy Spirit of God, for that Spirit is the seal with which you were marked for the day of our final liberation." So the Holy Spirit may be grieved, but you'll never grieve him away, for you have been sealed. The third may be obvious: the Holy Spirit is holy. As a believer, you can't just live a kind of slipshod life. He is a holy being, so if you go that route, you'll grieve Him.

I want to look at several questions, and each one begins with a "what." In fact, this message is about a five-what sermon. (That's about all the "whats" I generate, anyway.)

WHAT GRIEVES THE HOLY SPIRIT?

The psalmist recounted the experiences of the children of Israel in the wilderness:

> *How often they provoked Him in the wilderness, and grieved Him in the desert! Yes, again and again they tempted God, and limited the Holy One of Israel.* (Psalm 78:40–41 NKJV)

The children of Israel actually limited God because they grieved Him. So to grieve the Holy Spirit means that we limit God in our lives.

But what is it that causes the Spirit to be grieved? God Himself provided the answer when He said:

> *For forty years I was grieved with that generation, and said, "It is a people who go astray in their hearts, and they do not know My ways."* (Psalm 95:10 NKJV)

What was it that grieved God? It was the sins of the children of Israel. I want to confirm that.

Isaiah had something to say about this same experience:

> *But they rebelled and grieved His Holy Spirit; so He turned Himself against them as an enemy, and He fought against them.* (Isaiah 63:10 NKJV)

Isaiah specifically said that the children of Israel in the wilderness grieved the Holy Spirit of God.

Now let's move to the New Testament and look at a passage that really nails it down:

> *Therefore I was angry* [grieved] *with that generation, and said, "They always go astray in their heart, and they have not known My ways."* . . . *Now with whom was He angry* [grieved] *forty years? Was it not with those who sinned, whose corpses fell in the wilderness?* (Hebrews 3:10, 17 NKJV)

What is it that grieves the Holy Spirit of God? My beloved, it is sin. Sin grieves the Holy Spirit.

WHAT SIN GRIEVES THE HOLY SPIRIT?

Certainly it's true that *all* sin grieves the Spirit. But I want to deal with specifics and really make this clear, because a great many people attempt to evade and avoid this problem by saying they have gotten rid of their sin nature. Their argument is that the Holy Spirit couldn't dwell in a person who has a sin nature. May I say to you, Paul made it very clear that the Holy Spirit is able to dwell in a believer who has a sin nature. If He weren't capable of it, He wouldn't indwell *any* of us. Notice that Paul said:

> **For the death that He died, He died to sin once for all; but the life that He lives, He lives to God.** (Romans 6:10 NKJV)

Now let me give you my "McGee-icus ad absurdum" transla- tion: "For as to His dying, it was as to sin He died, once for all; but as to His living, it is as to God He lives." Paul was not saying here that Christ died for sin. He said that elsewhere, but here he was discussing the fact that Christ died a judg- ment death for our sin nature, and if He had not, then the Holy Spirit couldn't get within forty feet of any of us.

But, you see, He died not only *for* sin, but *to* sin. That's exactly what Paul meant in 2 Corinthians 5:21 (NKJV), "For He made Him who knew no sin to be sin for us, that we might become the righteousness of God in Him." On the cross, Christ became what we are (sinners) so that we today might be what He is.

My beloved, God has no notion of reforming the old nature. He put it to death on the cross, and when Christ died, He died to sin and your old nature was judged there. God has no notion of saving it. It's already judged, and when you die, it will go into the grave with you and never come out. (Won't you be glad to get rid of sinful old Vernon McGee? So will I. Oh, to get rid of him! And thank the Lord, we'll get rid of you, too, and I have a notion that you'll be happy for that.)

Because He died to sin for us, we are not to live unto that sin nature, but we are now to live unto Christ. Which leads me to say this: God has made provision for the prevention of sin in the life of the believer so that we might live triumphantly. But I also must agree with Dr. Scofield, who once said that although it is true that God has made ample provision, he had never met anyone who was living without sin. God's provision is perfect, but our entrance is imperfect because believers sin. We cannot get rid of our sin nature. He died to it, so you and I are to live conscious of the fact that we have that sin nature, but we are not to live *in* that sin nature. We are to live unto Christ.

Let's identify some of the sins of believers. What sins grieve the Holy Spirit? If everyone were given a chance to pick what he thinks is the worst sin, I know someone would say going to picture shows. Someone else would say dancing, and some others would say smoking. Really, I've looked, but I haven't found those verses. I say that for this reason: there are some folks today who say they don't do these things and, therefore, they are separated, spiritual Christians. Are you one of those?

Well, let's see. The Holy Spirit is called "the Spirit of truth," for our Lord Jesus said, "When He, the Spirit of truth, has come, He will guide you into all truth" (John 16:13 NKJV). And if He is the Spirit of truth, then one of the sins that would grieve Him would be lying, would it not?

The interesting thing is that so many people rip Ephesians 4:30 out and do not pay any attention to its context. Notice what comes after it:

> *And do not grieve the Holy Spirit of God, by whom you were sealed for the day of redemption. Let all bitterness, wrath, anger, clamor, and evil speaking be put away from you, with all malice.* (Ephesians 4:30–31 NKJV)

That's quite a list of sins that grieve the Holy Spirit!

And backing up a few verses, we read, "Therefore, putting away lying, 'Let each one of you speak truth with his neighbor,' for we are members of one another" (Ephesians 4:25 NKJV). If He's the Spirit of truth, then lying would grieve Him. Gossip also grieves the Holy Spirit of God, and where gossip is engaged in, the Holy Spirit of God cannot work in fullness of power. He's the Spirit of truth and any misrepresentation, any wagging tongue that says something that it cannot prove, grieves the Holy Spirit of God.

He is also called the "Spirit of wisdom" (Isaiah 11:2 NKJV), so a believer's ignorance of spiritual truths and the Word of God grieves the Holy Spirit. In fact, I personally believe that is what grieves the Holy Spirit more than anything else in our churches—the fact that men and women have been believers for ten or even fifty years, and yet they are still ignorant of the Word of God. They know practically nothing about it! But He's the Spirit of wisdom, and therefore ignorance grieves Him.

He has other titles as well. You may recall that Paul said in Romans 8:2 (NKJV), "For the law of the Spirit of life in Christ Jesus has made me free." So he is the Spirit of life. And, of course, He's the Spirit of power, "For God has not given us a spirit of fear, but of power and of love and of a sound mind" (2 Timothy 1:7 NKJV). Life and power! Did you know that a lukewarm, indifferent Christian hurts the cause of Christ more than ten infidels? He's the Spirit of life and of power, and when He's not moving in our hearts and lives giving life and power, then, my beloved, He's grieved.

Paul said in Romans 1:4 that He is "declared to be the Son of God with power according to the Spirit of holiness." Therefore, all impurity offends Him. There's more. Notice what else grieves, or offends, Him:

> *Let no corrupt word proceed out of your mouth, but what is good for necessary edification, that it may impart grace to the hearers. . . . Let all bitterness, wrath, anger, clamor, and evil speaking be put away from you, with all malice. . . . But fornication and all uncleanness or covetousness, let it not even be named among you.*
> (Ephesians 4:29, 31; 5:3 NKJV)

When you said that ugly thing about a certain person, were you really trying to "make a helpful suggestion," or were you motivated by malice? Are you money-hungry? We live in a world that has overworked sex—has that taken you down the drain today as a child of God? He's the Spirit of holiness, my friends, and we grieve Him when we engage in these things.

At this point, you may think I'm meddling, maybe even stepping on your toes, and ought to stop. But, may I say to you, these are the sins that are clearly identified in the Word of God, and they grieve the Holy Spirit. It's not all of them, but these are things that fundamental Christians are doing today. That's one of the reasons why we are not seeing a great manifestation of the Spirit of God today; it's because many believers have grieved the Spirit of God, and He cannot work in our midst.

WHAT HAPPENS WHEN A CHRISTIAN SINS?

When a Christian sins, he doesn't lose his salvation. Remember, until that day when we are presented to Christ, we've been sealed by the Holy Spirit. Our salvation is not in danger. We may not lose our salvation when we grieve the Holy Spirit by sinning, but we do lose our fellowship. We are told that Satan came into the Upper Room through the heart of Judas Iscariot (see John 13:2), and because of his presence, fellowship was broken in the Upper Room.

So our Lord arose and began to wash the disciples' feet. But Peter said, "Don't wash my feet" (see John 13:8). Peter was a man who was susceptible to Satan. We know from the past that our Lord had said to him, "Get behind Me, Satan" (Matthew 16:23 NKJV). So in the Upper Room, Jesus said to Simon Peter, "If I do not wash you, you have no part [fellowship] with Me" (John 13:8 NKJV). In other words, "You have to be clean if you're going to have fellowship with Me."

Oh, how believers today think that they can have fellowship with Christ with sin in their lives—it's impossible! When there is sin in the life of a believer, he loses his fellowship.

> *If we say that we have fellowship with Him, and walk in darkness, we lie and do not practice the truth.* (1 John 1:6 NKJV)

There's no power, there's no fruit of the Spirit in the life, he is miserable, and he makes everybody around him miserable. He becomes critical, cantankerous, difficult, the darkness of the world makes an assault upon the soul of the believer, and it intrudes into his life. The joy of the Lord is gone, and he has to seek for satisfaction in the things of the world. Before long, those around him say he's living just like the man in the world, and to all outward appearances, he is.

My beloved, believers are divided into two categories. There is one category of those who are living with a grieved Holy Spirit, and there is another category of folks who are living with the ungrieved Holy Spirit.

WHAT MUST A BELIEVER DO?

A believer cannot continue in sin without serious consequences. Not only is fellowship with God lost, but something else is going to happen: he'll find that God will move in and deal with him. But a believer can do something about his sin. May I say, Scripture is crystal clear at this point:

> *If we confess our sins, He is faithful and just to forgive us our sins and to cleanse us from all unrighteousness.* (1 John 1:9 NKJV*)*

Obviously, John was speaking here to believers, not unbelievers. I say this very carefully, but if you've never accepted Christ as your Savior, God is not asking you to do this. He's not saying to you, "Confess your sins." He's saying to you, "Believe on the Lord Jesus Christ, and you will be saved" (Acts 16:31 NKJV).

But if believers want to have fellowship and we confess our sins, "He is faithful and just to forgive us our sins and to cleanse us from all unrighteousness." The believer is to do just one thing: confess. God does two things: He forgives, and He cleanses.

WHAT IS GENUINE CONFESSION?

But what does it mean to have genuine confession of sin? May I say to you that there is more in Scripture on this particular subject than any other. The Old Testament Book of Joshua records a classic example. God had just enabled the children of Israel to take the city of Jericho. Fresh with victory, Joshua thought he could send a little army up to the city of Ai and take it as well. But Joshua's army met defeat and, believe me, it was humiliation. So much so that Joshua went before God and said:

> *Alas, Lord GOD, why have You brought this people over the Jordan at all—to deliver us into the hand of the Amorites, to destroy us? Oh, that we had been content, and dwelt on the other side of the Jordan! O Lord, what shall I say when Israel turns its back before its enemies? For the Canaanites and all the inhabitants of the land will hear it, and surround us, and cut off our name from the earth. Then what will You do for Your great name?*
> (Joshua 7:7-9 NKJV)

Oh, Joshua, he prayed about everything but the right thing. He said, "What will the Canaanites think? What will happen to us?" But he didn't deal with sin. So the Lord said to him, "Get up off your face, and quit your whining and sniveling—this is no time to pray" (see Joshua 7:10).

Am I saying that the saints shouldn't pray? No! But there are times when you should pray, and there are other times when you should get to the root of the problem and straighten things out. What was wrong in this situation? "Israel has sinned" (Joshua 7:11 NKJV). That was the problem: sin.

> *And they have also transgressed My covenant which I*
> *commanded them. For they have even taken some of the*
> *accursed things, and have both stolen and deceived; and*
> *they have also put it among their own stuff.* (Joshua
> 7:11 NKJV)

Joshua had to get that sin ferreted out and dealt with.
When the guilty party, Achan, was finally found, he con-
fessed to Joseph by listing each and every thing he had stolen
or done wrong (see Joshua 7:20–21). Believers, true confession does not deal in generalities. Spell it out as Achan did.
Tell God everything that is in your heart—just open it up to
Him and tell Him exactly what your sin is. That is confession. There can be no joy, no power, and no victory in your
life until there is confession of sin.

Now, what happened to Achan?

> *And Joshua said, "Why have you troubled us? The LORD*
> *will trouble you this day." So all Israel stoned him with*
> *stones; and they burned them with fire after they had*
> *stoned them with stones.* (Joshua 7:25 NKJV)

You may think that was harsh, but God has not changed; He
does the same thing today. Will you notice this: "For if you
live according to the flesh you will die" (Romans 8:13 NKJV).
Physically, no. Spiritually, no. Then what does it mean? If
you continue in sin, you are going to die to fellowship with
God. Your life will be as dead as a dodo bird. Sin kills, my
beloved, and it has to be dealt with.

Listen to Him:

Therefore put to death your members which are on the earth: fornication, uncleanness, passion, evil desire, and covetousness, which is idolatry. (Colossians 3:5 NKJV)

May I urge you to commit a murder? Would you take that member of your body that's causing you to offend and crucify it? You can't crucify your body, but you can deal with that tongue that gets you in trouble by talking too much. Take it before the Lord and confess it. Achan had to come out in the open and say, "I saw it, I coveted it, I kept it." That's true confession of sin. You've got to deal with it, friend. This business today of saying, "Lord, forgive me my sins," and then hopping up off our knees to go out and do the same sin just so we can come back and confess again, that's no good—that's not confession of sins.

The Corinthian church was in a city given over to immorality and all kinds of funny religions. Believe me, that church got in a mess. When Paul wrote his first letter to the Corinthians, there were divisions, lawsuits, and immorality. There was sin regarding the Lord's Table, sin regarding giving, and sin regarding marriage. And do you think God shut his eyes to all of that? No. God chastened, as Paul told them, "For this reason many are weak and sick among you, and many sleep" (1 Corinthians 11:30 NKJV). In order for God to remove the whip from their backs, they had to deal with the sin.

For if we would judge ourselves, we would not be judged. But when we are judged, we are chastened by the Lord, that we may not be condemned with the world. (1 Corinthians 11:31–32 NKJV)

My Christian friend, to confess your sin means that you judge it yourself. "Confess" is the Greek word *homologeo*, which means to come over on God's side, look at yourself, and recognize what He recognizes—that you are a dirty low-down sinner. Then offer Him no excuse whatsoever, but say to Him, "Here is my sin, black as it is; but I want fellowship with You, so I claim the blood of Christ." My friend, when a child of God sins, there ought to be an agony of soul and tears of sorrow. If not, something is wrong.

What did the Corinthians do about their sin? Friends, they did something about it. The fact of the matter is that they did everything about it! They straightened out the immorality, the divisions—everything. When Paul wrote them a second letter, he said:

Now I rejoice, not that you were made sorry, but that your sorrow led to repentance. For you were made sorry in a godly manner, that you might suffer loss from us in nothing. For godly sorrow produces repentance leading to salvation, not to be regretted; but the sorrow of the world produces death. For observe this very thing, that you sorrowed in a godly manner: What diligence it produced in you, what clearing of yourselves, what indignation, what fear, what vehement desire, what zeal, what vindication!

In all things you proved yourselves to be clear in this matter. (2 Corinthians 7:9–11 NKJV)

When the sin was called to their attention, they sorrowed, dealt with it, and then made it right. And if there isn't that agony of soul, it's not true confession.

After confession comes repentance, which means to turn from the sin. You see, the prodigal always comes home. Always. He comes home because he's out of fellowship with his Father, and that brings agony of soul and shedding of tears. May I say to you, no child of God can go on in sin. If you can go on living in sin and it does not affect you in any way, then you are not a child of God. You can't be.

The child of God will sin, but when he sins, he'll confess it to the Father. Once there has been confession and repentance, the Holy Spirit is no longer grieved, fellowship is restored, and the Spirit brings light and power to the believer's life.

Chapter 12

THE FRUIT OF
THE SPIRIT

When I was a boy living in west Texas, a drought was a regular and annual phase of nature. There is the old bromide that nothing is sure but death and taxes. But out in Texas, there were three things sure: death, taxes, and a drought every summer.

My father seemed to have the habit of waiting until the weather was the driest and then writing in and asking for a nursery catalog. Even to this day, I can see those colored pictures in the catalog of the delicious apples. I have never seen an apple that really looks like those pictures, but they were certainly pretty in the catalog.

One time, my father ordered several of those apple trees, and, I must confess, I was disappointed on their arrival. They were scrawny, anemic-looking little trees. We put those trees out, watered them, and nursed them through the hot summer, waiting for the apples. The trees made it through nicely because we watered them very well. But the second summer was too much for them, and all of them laid down and died. Honestly, to this good day, I'm not sure they were apple trees at all, because the only way you can know would be to get apples, and we never did.

Now I want to look at another fruit catalog—this catalog is of the fruit that should be growing in the life of a Christian. If you are a child of God, there should be lovely fruit growing in your life. The most important phase of the Christian life is fruit bearing. Our Lord said to His own yonder in the Upper Room:

> *By this My Father is glorified, that you bear much fruit; so you will be My disciples . . . You did not choose Me, but I chose you and appointed you that you should go and bear fruit, and that your fruit should remain, that whatever you ask the Father in My name He may give you.* (John 15:8, 16 NKJV)

This is a very wonderful passage of Scripture. Our Lord said that the reason He chose you, the reason why you're a child of God through faith, and the reason that He has not taken you home is so that you might bear fruit in this world. That is your purpose. May I say to you, He even puts it down as the condition to hearing and answering prayer! If you and I are fruit-bearing Christians, whatever we ask, He will do— that is a tremendous statement, my beloved.

So let's look at this fruit. In God's Word, you can identify the fruit that He says should be growing in the lives of believers just as easily as choosing fruit trees from a nursery catalog. But let me hasten to say that the fruit is not soul winning. I hear many say that we have been saved in order that we might win others. I believe that is true, but winning others is really the by-product of having fruit. Also, some folk say we are saved to serve, but God doesn't say that. He says the important thing is that we bear fruit.

Nor is the fruit leadership. Someone once told me that the problem in the church today is that we have more chiefs than we have Indians—everybody wants to be a chief, and very few want to be Indians. Because we've emphasized leadership so much, some think they are not even living the Christian life unless they are the leader of something. Well, may I say, fruit is not leadership.

So what is the fruit? Let's do something better than turn the pages of the catalog—let's go straight to the orchard and examine the fruit that is in the life of the believer. Now, if you were not raised in the country, I think I should warn you that there is something else that grows in the orchard; you see, there's always something else that tries to overcome the fruit. In fact, there is a struggle going on in nature.

I once lost an apricot tree in my orchard out in Pasadena. (My lot is just seventy-two feet wide and 123 feet deep, but I like to think of it as a ranch.) I had quite a few trees, and I think what caused it to die was that it had too much competition. There were other things trying to grow, and it had too many enemies. There are today in nature slugs and bugs and stinkweeds that attempt to crowd out the fruit. And in the life of the believer, there are always things that will attempt to crowd out the fruit of the Spirit. In other words, it's quite possible that the weeds will grow and the fruit will not be produced.

Paul spoke of that very thing:

> *For the flesh lusts* [I would say "wars"] *against the Spirit, and the Spirit against the flesh; and these are contrary to one another, so that you do not do the things that you wish.* (Galatians 5:17 NKJV)

The flesh wants to have its way and is actually in competition against the Holy Spirit. So there is a danger of producing something besides fruit. And that which the flesh produces is not something that God can use; it's not fruit at all.

Paul himself experienced that struggle: "For what I will to do [the new man wanted to produce fruit], that I do not practice [the old nature would not do it]" (Romans 7:15 NKJV). You can be a child of God and be producing works of the flesh in your life, and if you are, you are not living by the Spirit of God. And I can tell you, if the works of the flesh are appearing in your life, you are a discontented and trouble-making child of God.

The Law was given to control the flesh; it was never given to produce the fruits of the Spirit. "But if you are led by the Spirit, you are not under the law" (Galatians 5:18 NKJV). The fruits of the Spirit are something else other than the works of the Law. But the Law was given to hold the flesh in check.

Unfortunately, when the flesh is not held in check in the lives of believers, the works of the flesh appear, and it is an ugly, loathsome brood:

> *Now the works of the flesh are evident, which are: adultery, fornication, uncleanness, lewdness, idolatry, sorcery, hatred, contentions, jealousies, outbursts of wrath, selfish ambitions, dissensions, heresies, envy, murders, drunkenness, revelries, and the like.* (Galatians 5:19–21 NKJV)

If you are living in the flesh, these are the things that are being produced in your life. But if you are going to have the fruits of the Spirit, you can't produce these works of the flesh at all. For these things will lead to tragedy, failure as a Christian, unhappiness, and trouble.

Paul, you see, was speaking to believers when he said:

> *Do not be deceived, God is not mocked; for whatever a man sows, that he will also reap. For he who sows to his flesh will of the flesh reap corruption, but he who sows to the Spirit will of the Spirit reap everlasting life.* (Galatians 6:7–8 NKJV)

I personally believe that's a law of God, just like the law of gravity. If a farmer sows corn, you can be sure that he'll reap corn. If he sows wheat, he'll reap wheat. My friend, as a believer, if you are sowing to the flesh, you "will of the flesh reap corruption." There is no way around it.

Now, the child of God does not have to produce these

things. These are the works of the flesh, but a believer can produce the fruit of the Spirit. God has another principle:

> *But the fruit of the Spirit is love, joy, peace, longsuffering, kindness, goodness, faithfulness, gentleness, self-control. Against such there is no law.* (Galatians 5:22–23 NKJV)

You can't produce these fruits by following the Law; in fact, there is not one of these lovely fruits that you can produce on your own. We are totally incapable; they can be produced only by the Holy Spirit. "For the fruit of the Spirit," Paul said in Ephesians 5:9 (NKJV), "is in all goodness, righteousness, and truth." You can know whether you are living by the flesh or living in the power, in the fullness, of the Holy Spirit by seeing if He is producing these fruits in your life.

So let's examine this fruit.

LOVE

First, the fruit of the Spirit is love. That's not bad grammar. He didn't mean to say that the fruit of the Spirit *are* love, joy, peace, etc. It is love, for from love stem all of these others. Love is the most important one of all, and it's primary here because that's the thing that only the Spirit of God can produce in your life—love not only for God, but for other believers. Did our Lord say, "By this all will know that you are My disciples, if you are fundamental in the faith"? No. I wish He had, but He didn't say that. "By this all will know that you are My disciples, if you're a member of such-and-such church"? My heavens, no. He said, "By this all will know that you are My disciples, if you have love for one another" (John 13:35 NKJV).

My friend, only the Holy Spirit of God can give you this kind of love. The only love that you and I are capable of is selfish or sexual love—that's the only kind we can manifest. Only the Holy Spirit can manifest in us the love of God.

I believe in the security of the believer, but I also believe that there are a great many Christians who do not have the assurance of their salvation. The reason is because of their antipathy, hatred, bitterness, and criticism of other believers. John wrote, "We know that we have passed from death to life, because we love the brethren. He who does not love his brother abides in death" (1 John 3:14 NKJV). I do not know how anything can be clearer than that. If you are a child of God and you are hating another believer, you're in death. Because the Holy Spirit, when He's indwelling a believer, produces love in the heart for every other believer.

This is rather heart-searching, is it not? If only this lovely fruit were on exhibit today. These great fruit markets here in California like to put all their best fruit on display; wouldn't it be wonderful if the church could put on display this fruit of love among the brethren?

JOY

Paul said to the Romans, "For the kingdom of God is not eating and drinking, but righteousness and peace and joy in the Holy Spirit" (Romans 14:17 NKJV). That kind of joy does not depend on circumstances, but on the working of the Holy Spirit within.

When Paul was in prison in Rome, he wrote to the Philippians, "Rejoice in the Lord always. Again I will say, rejoice!" (Philippians 4:4 NKJV). Oh, my Christian friend, many of us today lose our joy as soon as the way gets a little difficult, the going gets bad, and the day gets dark. As a child of God, you should have the Holy Spirit producing joy in your life; this is the most valuable thing in the world you can have.

Let me clarify that this kind of joy is not some "everybody smile" philosophy. Smiling doesn't prove anything. You are not to go around with a smile like a Cheshire cat all the time to prove you're a Christian. Joy is not something that's rubbed on the face; it's something that's in the heart.

Actually, there are times when we can be sorrowing but at the same time rejoicing. Look at our Lord, who was "a Man of sorrows and acquainted with grief" (Isaiah 53:3 NKJV), and yet we are told He was anointed "with the oil of gladness" above His companions (Hebrews 1:9 NKJV). He even said to His own yonder in the Upper Room, "These things I have spoken to you, that My joy may remain in you, and that your joy may be full" (John 15:11 NKJV). He wants you to rejoice, and you can't rejoice in the circumstances down here unless the Spirit of God is producing fruit in your heart and life.

PEACE

The next fruit is peace—peace of heart, peace in the storms of life, the kind of peace our Lord had.

Peace I leave with you, My peace I give to you; not as the world gives do I give to you. Let not your heart be troubled, neither let it be afraid. (John 14:27 NKJV)

Oh, how I've wanted that peace! You may recall the storm on the little Sea of Galilee, and how the disciples, who were fisherman accustomed to the sea, said, "This little boat cannot ride out this storm." And where was Jesus? Asleep in the boat (see Mark 4:38). Anybody can sleep when there is no storm, but we need the kind of peace that captures our hearts when the storm is blowing.

Years ago, there was a contest for artists to present a picture that would best set forth the concept of peace. Many wonderful pictures were presented by many outstanding artists. One was of a very calm sea with a boat on it, its sails unfurled. That certainly is a picture of peace. Another artist painted a picture of sheep grazing in a peaceful meadow without a thing to disturb or bother them. The interesting thing is that those two pictures did not win the prize. The one that won the prize was a picture of a craggy mountainside, and there was a storm blowing, the likes of which you've never seen before. There was a little old scrawny bush stuck out of a rock, and in that little bush was a nest, and in that nest was a mother bird sitting on some eggs. That storm was blowing and that little mother bird was just sitting there, as calm as you please, riding out the storm. That's the kind of peace that the Holy Spirit produces—the kind of peace that endures when the storms begin to beat in upon our little bark.

My, how that fruit is needed today in the lives of believers. And it's impossible for us to produce it. Only the Spirit of God can produce this in our lives.

LONG-SUFFERING

Long-suffering means patience, endurance, and you will find that the Word of God has a great deal to say about this.

> *For whatever things were written before were written for our learning, that we through the patience and comfort of the Scriptures might have hope. Now may the God of patience and comfort grant you to be like-minded toward one another, according to Christ Jesus.* (Romans 15:4–5 NKJV)

The reason God gave us these stories in the Old Testament is for our patience. Some of us fail so often, and we get impatient and say, "I'm going to walk out on all of it." But read the story of Jacob and you won't walk out, because you'll learn from Jacob that God won't walk out on you. God gave us that story to make us patient. Maybe one of the reasons why we're not as patient as we should be is because we haven't read the Old Testament enough. That is given for our consolation and for our patience.

Knowing that the testing of your faith produces patience. But let patience have its perfect work, that you may be perfect and complete, lacking nothing. (James 1:3–4 NKJV)

KINDNESS

I move on to the next fruit. My, this is a lovely display of fruit that God has for us. Kindness, which actually means graciousness. To be completely honest, it means good manners. A real born-again child of God will be courteous; that's a fruit of the Spirit.

The South used to be covered with private schools that did nothing in the world but pass on southern culture and manners. I am sorry to have to say that good manners are passing from our culture today, because we thought we could just teach it to folk. But it doesn't come out that way. It's a fruit of the Holy Spirit, and the only thing that can make you truly well mannered is the Spirit of God manifesting fruit in your life.

GOODNESS

The next fruit is goodness. There are a lot of believers, you know who they are, who have never done anything spectacular, never served on a board, never occupied a prominent place, never been leaders, but they are simply good people. Do you know that's a fruit of the Holy Spirit?

FAITHFULNESS

Faithfulness is fidelity, dependability. Only the Holy Spirit of God can make you dependable. I once knew a lovely teacher in the Sunday school. She taught for thirty-two years and never missed a Sunday. That's faithfulness, my beloved. And only the Holy Spirit of God can make you faithful. The reason why there are so many believers you can't depend on is because the Holy Spirit alone can make us dependable and faithful to a task.

GENTLENESS

Meekness is gentleness, but meekness is not weakness. It doesn't mean that a Christian ought to be a Mr. Milquetoast. It really just means the opposite of brutality or cruelty. That is, to be strong without being brutal.

I say this reverently, but our Lord was an extrovert. He went into the temple, said, "Get out of here," and those people got out. And yet He said, "I am gentle and lowly" (Matthew 11:29 NKJV). He was not weak. Today, a great many people think that being a Christian means having to compromise on everything. My friend, a child of God is one who will stand for what is right. That happens to be meekness—being able to stand for that which is right.

SELF-CONTROL

We come to the last one—self-control. The King James Version calls it "temperance." Paul said:

> *And everyone who competes for the prize is temperate in all*
> *things. Now they do it to obtain a perishable crown, but we*
> *for an imperishable crown.* (1 Corinthians 9:25 NKJV)

A man who is in training for an athletic event is going to let certain things alone, not because they are wrong, but because he is in training. Paul said, "As a Christian, I am in training. And since I am in training, in order that I might win a crown, there are certain things I don't do."

Don't tell me that certain things are wrong and certain things are right. That's not the standard for a believer. The standard for a believer is, "Do I want to please Him? Do I want to hear His approval? Do I want to 'lay aside every weight, and the sin which so easily ensnares [me], and . . . run with endurance the race that is set before [me], looking unto Jesus, the author and finisher of our faith' [Hebrews 12:1–2 NKJV]? Do I really want to win?"

If you want to win, it's not a question of right and wrong. Don't go out to the football field and tell those boys that it is wrong to eat pie, because it's not wrong to eat pie. But when you're in training for football, you don't eat pie. It's not being wrong; you're just not going to make the team if you eat pie.

And for a child of God, it's not a question of things being right and wrong; it's a question of whether you want to please Him. It's a question of whether you want to live for God or not. That puts it on a different plane.

Isn't this lovely fruit? Don't you wish you could have a dozen of these nine wonderful fruits? Others have said that the fruit present a minibiography of the life of Christ. That is true, but they should be manifest in the life of a believer. Some folk try to act cultured and refined, but that's not the way to do it. A child of God needs to be filled with the Holy Spirit—it's His fruit and He provides it.

Our Lord said:

> *You will know them by their fruits. Do men gather grapes from thornbushes or figs from thistles? Even so, every good tree bears good fruit, but a bad tree bears bad fruit. A good tree cannot bear bad fruit, nor can a bad tree bear good fruit. Every tree that does not bear good fruit is cut down and thrown into the fire. Therefore by their fruits you will know them.* (Matthew 7:16–20 NKJV)

Someone may claim to have trusted in Christ, but his neighbor next door doesn't know and the man he works with doesn't know. The only way in the world for people to know is by the fruit. "By their fruits you will know them."

Chapter 13

THE WILL OF GOD AND QUENCHING THE SPIRIT

As Paul concluded his first letter to the Thessalonians, he put down commandments for believers. One of these is expressed in just a few brief words:

Do not quench the Spirit. (1 Thessalonians 5:19 NKJV)

This wonderful verse needs to be taken into our homes, places of business, and schools today! We have already put on display the fruit of the Spirit. The motive in doing that was the same as what prompts the supermarket to put up front an attractive display of fruits and vegetables: to create a desire that leads to an effort to possess the fruit. But there is a price tag on the fruit of the Spirit. I want to be very candid: the fruit of the Spirit is rather expensive.

It is said that Henry Drummond, the Scottish lecturer

and writer, once remarked, "Salvation is free; the admission fee is nothing. But the dues are rather expensive." May I say to you, being saved costs you nothing; the price has been paid. But if you want to have the fruit of the Spirit, you'll have to pay a tremendous price for it. In fact, there are certain commands in connection with the Holy Spirit that the believer must carry out before there can be the fruit of the Spirit in his life. One such command is this: "Do not quench the Spirit."

One of the figures used in the Word of God for the Holy Spirit is fire. On the Day of Pentecost, the Holy Spirit descended not as actual fire, but "*as of* fire" (Acts 2:3 NKJV), meaning "like" fire. Also, it was the Holy Spirit appearing as a pillar of fire that led the children of Israel by night. Keeping that in mind, consider that "to quench" means "to suppress or stifle," as we see here:

> **Above all, taking the shield of faith with which you will be able to quench all the fiery darts of the wicked one.**
> (Ephesians 6:16 NKJV)

The Holy Spirit is spoken of as a fire in the metaphorical sense. A fire possesses and consumes anything over which it has control until it is quenched, until it is stifled, until it is suppressed. So when Paul says, "Do not quench the Spirit," he is telling us to not put the Spirit out, don't extinguish Him.

Then what does it mean to quench, or extinguish, the Holy Spirit? It is to resist His leading. It is when a believer says no to God. It is putting the will of the individual above the will of God. That is what it means to quench the Holy Spirit.

Now, that was the condition of each of us at some point since, fundamentally, that is what it means to be a lost person, a sinner. Isaiah expressed our basic problem when he said:

> *All we like sheep have gone astray; we have turned, every one, to his own way; and the LORD has laid on Him the iniquity of us all.* (Isaiah 53:6 NKJV)

Our problem is that little phrase, "his own way"—each one has turned to his own way. That is what Paul meant when he said:

> *Because the carnal mind is enmity against God; for it is not subject to the law of God, nor indeed can be. So then those who are in the flesh cannot please God.* (Romans 8:7–8 NKJV)

Why? Because in our old nature there is one thing that is uppermost. We want to have our own way. Your old nature may let you be religious—you can even become the most pious person you've ever seen—as long as you let the old nature have his way. That's our problem.

Jeremiah put it like this: "O LORD, I know the way of man is not in himself; it is not in man who walks to direct his own steps" (Jeremiah 10:23 NKJV). Man is totally incapable of directing his steps as God has ordered them, because that old nature wants its own way. Unfortunately for the old nature,

"There is a way that seems right to a man, but its end is the way of death" (Proverbs 14:12 NKJV).

When you are born again, become a child of God, you are given a new nature. That new nature can obey God.

For those who live according to the flesh set their minds on the things of the flesh, but those who live according to the Spirit, [they will mind or obey] *the things of the Spirit.* (Romans 8:5 NKJV)

A child of God is given a nature whereby he can obey God; but when that child of God will not obey God, he quenches the Holy Spirit.

That puts most of us as believers on the horns of a dilemma. Our Lord expressed it like this:

No one can serve two masters; for either he will hate the one and love the other, or else he will be loyal to the one and despise the other. You cannot serve God and mammon. (Matthew 6:24 NKJV)

Many of us are trying to do both. My, how pious we are on Sundays, but you ought to see us during the week—then we are not quite so pious or well pleasing to God. But my friend, you can't do both, for "a double-minded man [is] unstable in all his ways" (James 1:8 NKJV). You have to drop on one side or the other.

The believer must choose the will of God, and that means renouncing self-will. Reduced to this very simple statement, it means to say yes to God and to yield to Him. But I need to add something here. Paul said to the Roman believers:

> *And do not present* [yield] *your members as instruments of unrighteousness to sin, but present* [yield] *yourselves to God as being alive from the dead, and your members as instruments of righteousness to God.* (Romans 6:13 NKJV)

The meaning in the original Greek is not that we ought to yield ourselves time and time again. Rather, once and for all we ought to yield ourselves to God.

My, how this is misunderstood today. A great many people think, *Now in this particular matter, I'd like to have God's will.* It doesn't mean that. It means making the will of God the rule of all your life from here on out. It applies to the minutest details of your life as well as to the big decisions that you make. Once and for all you must present, or yield, yourself to God to do His will.

It doesn't mean to know His will; it means to accept by faith the will of God and be in total submission to Him. It's not a question of doing the will of God in one particular thing or another, but will you do the will of God in anything and everything? That's what it means to yield, and until you and I have done that, we are quenching the Holy Spirit in our lives.

After a few years of experience, I'm confident that the problem of believers today is not knowing the will of God. Here is the real problem: will you do the will of God when you know it? Most of us think the will of God is like going to a department store and making a purchase. We want to examine the material. If we like it, we buy it; if we don't like it, we put it back on the shelf. But God says we must choose His will without knowing it—by faith—and *then* He'll reveal the step-by-step process to us.

I believe the problem of 99.44 percent of believers is this: we never made the decision back yonder to accept God's will in every aspect of our entire lives. Instead, we wait until we get into a tight place, and then if God's will reveals a nice little easy way out, then we're sure glad to have it. But that's not the will of God. His will is for you to elect to say to Him, "I'll do *anything* You want me to do."

And, my friend, God is able to make a willing soul know His will. Our problem is that we want to know it beforehand, and that's just not the way He does it. Never does He do it that way! He always speaks to those who have chosen to make the will of God the rule of their lives.

The Lord Jesus Christ is the perfect illustration of this. Paul even wrote, "Let this mind be in you which was also in Christ Jesus" (Philippians 2:5 NKJV). Now what kind of a mind is that? I hate to hear people sing songs along the lines of "I will go where You want me to go, dear Lord. I'll be what You want me to be, I'll do what You want me to do." So few mean it! There's a proviso that they do not sing: "Provided it's according to my way, provided I like it, and provided it fits into my program." My friend, today the Lord Jesus Christ is our perfect example of one who made the will of God the rule of His life. Someone has said that God had only one Son, and He was a missionary. Our Lord could say truthfully, "I'll go where You want me to go, be what You want me to be, and do what You want Me to do." The writer to the Hebrews put it like this:

> *Then I said, "Behold, I have come—in the volume of the book it is written of Me—to do Your will, O God."* (Hebrews 10:7 NKJV)

And at another time, our Lord Himself said:

> *For I have come down from heaven, not to do My own will, but the will of Him who sent Me.* (John 6:38 NKJV)

Now, let's go back to Philippians 2:5, and will you notice that Paul said, "*Let* this mind be in you." It's not a command; you're not asked to do some great thing, make some great stride, or make some great effort. "*Let* this mind be in you." It's a matter of submission, of obedience, and of not quenching the Holy Spirit. It's saying yes to God.

How can you translate the will of God into your life? I do not claim to be exhausting this subject, but I can suggest three things that are in the Word of God.

DESIRE HIS WILL

First of all, there must be a desire for the will of God in your life. I believe that it must be a consuming passion, desired above everything else in life.

I'll be very candid and say that if you're a satisfied, comfortable Christian, you might as well stop reading right now because the rest of this message is wasted as far as you are concerned. A lot of saints today are like Israel. Moses wrote:

> *But Jeshurun* [Israel] *grew fat and kicked; you grew fat, you grew thick, you are obese! Then he forsook God who made him, and scornfully esteemed the Rock of his salvation.* (Deuteronomy 32:15 KJV)

And that's not all. God said, according to the King James Version:

> *For Israel slideth back as a backsliding heifer . . . Let him alone.* (Hosea 4:16–17 KJV)

Believer, are you grown fat and kicking? Are you a backsliding heifer? Isn't that an awful expression? A great many people think it means to slide backwards, but it doesn't. I thank the Lord I used to have to milk three cows when I was a boy. One was an old mule-y cow, and she had the meanest calf that you've ever seen. Mean! I'd let the calf in for a while to be with its momma, but then it would come time to lead the calf out. Have you ever tried to get a mean old calf to do something it doesn't want to do? That little heifer would put her two front feet down just so, and I'd have to skid her along like a sled. That's backsliding—not doing the will!

Israel was a backsliding heifer. She bowed her little old head, she stuck her feet to the ground, and she was as stubborn as a mule. A lot of Christians are just like that. But I learned a secret: if you twist the tail, my, they will move forward. But God said, "Let him alone. Do nothing" (see Hosea 4:17). You see, God won't even do that if you are not willing. Knowing and following the will of God is for those who are willing.

When Saul of Tarsus was converted, the first thing he said to the Lord was, "What do You want me to do?" (Acts 9:6 NKJV). That became the rule of his life. As I've said, the will of God is not necessarily the easy way out. The point I'm trying to make is that regardless of what it is, are you willing to do it? No conditions, no "if," no "but," no "perhaps"—are you willing to do God's will in total submission?

I wish we had more dedicated Christians today who have no plan and program for themselves, but are willing to do His will. The reason today why there are so many Christians out of fellowship with God is because when you quench the Holy Spirit, you lose your fellowship with Him.

God has power to place you in His path. A great many people said, "Oh, if I could only get here or I could only do that." If you really want God's will, submit to Him, for He has the power to put you in His will. Not only that, but He knows what's best for each of us. He has equipped these bodies and minds with everything except a steering wheel. On our own, we don't even know what a day will bring forth, and so we cannot plan. But may I say to you, God knows what's best for each one of us, and He has the power to place us in His will.

I'm amazed at these men and women who have traveled

through space. But I tell you, when they step into their spacecrafts, they are no longer in control. Someone else directs every move until they get back down to terra firma. That's what it means to be in the will of God: He's controlling every move of your life.

God loves you, and He wants you in His will. Oh, we've all heard someone say, "I'd yield to God, but I know what He'd do. He'd pick me up and put me down in a swamp in the middle of Africa, and I don't want that." May I say, when you say something like that, you are saying that God is a hard taskmaster. He's not! God loves you, and His will for you is the best thing in your life. If He wants you in a swamp in Africa, that's the only place in the world where you'll be happy. But if He doesn't want you there and wants you somewhere else instead, that is the only place you'll be happy. He loves you, and He'll pick the best thing for you.

Oh, my friend, today we need to have a desire, an overweening passion, for the will of God. Until we have that, we haven't even gotten to first base with Him.

KNOWLEDGE OF THE WORD OF GOD

The second requirement for knowing and doing His will is a knowledge of the Word of God. Paul wrote to the Colossians:

> *For this reason we also, since the day we heard it, do not cease to pray for you, and to ask that you may be filled*

with the knowledge of His will in all wisdom and spiritual understanding. (Colossians 1:9 NKJV)

What is "the knowledge of His will"? May I say to you, it's His Word. Paul prayed that believers might be filled with the Word of God.

Someone has defined sin as any transgression of the Law of God. That's not adequate, because we do not find all the will of God in the Law of God. But we do find it in the Word of God. So sin today is to fall short of what He wants, and you won't get that, friends, anywhere else except in His Word. Therefore, the Holy Spirit will never lead contrary to the Word, but He will always lead in accordance to the Word of God.

A great many people try to use the Word of God as a sort of Ouija board. They get into a particular circumstance, and then they go to the Bible and begin thumbing through it. They find a nice comforting verse and say, "That's what God gave me." I'm always suspicious when someone says God has "given" him a verse. How did he get it? God is not giving out verses like shuffling cards. He gives the *whole* Word of God.

You can't just go to the Word of God and pick out one little verse. What do you think this is, Las Vegas? This is not a gamble! You must know the Word of God, my beloved. The Bible is not a spare tire or a first aid kit; it's a chart and compass. In fact, the Word is God's radar screen.

We sometimes get a thick layer of fog right around the Los Angeles airport. When that happens, does the pilot in the incoming plane say to the person in the tower, "I'm coming in, but I don't want you taking over. Just tell me 'right' or 'left,' and I'll do it myself"? Is that the way they do it? No, but that's the way a lot of Christians are trying to do it: "Lord, I want to do it myself, so You just tell me if I should go right or left at this particular point." But God doesn't do it that way. When the plane comes in through the fog, the pilot gets in position and then the person in the tower looks at the radar and says, "I'll take over. You are in my control. Higher, more to the left, come down, down, down."

My friend, that's what it means to know the will of God. If you have His radar screen (the Word) before you all the time as a chart and compass, you will grow in grace and knowledge of Him. In order to see through the fog and discern His will, we must have a comprehensive knowledge of the Word of God.

And in order to understand it, we must have the Holy Spirit. Paul wrote:

> *Now we have received, not the spirit of the world, but the Spirit who is from God, that we might know the things that have been freely given to us by God.* (1 Corinthians 2:12 NKJV)

A most glorious privilege you and I have as believers is a book that the Holy Spirit alone can interpret for us and make real in our lives. You and I can never know the will of God, ignorant of the Word of God. That's the reason why a great many believers are cruising in a fog, totally ignorant of the Word of God. He's the author of the Book, and He alone can interpret it to our hearts and lives.

Sanctified Common Sense

Lastly, we must use sanctified common sense. You know, the Christian life is not lived by rule and rote, for "where the Spirit of the Lord is, there is liberty" (2 Corinthians 3:17 NKJV). You and I today depend too much on circumstances. I know that as I look back on my own life, I, like Gideon, have worn out about twenty-five fleeces by putting them out and squeezing water from them (see Judges 6:36–40). My friend, God is not leading us by fleeces. He leads today by the Holy Spirit who dwells within us.

Paul said:

> *Work out your own salvation with fear and trembling; for it is God who works in you both to will and to do for His good pleasure.* (Philippians 2:12–13 NKJV)

Instead of running around looking at the fleece, I tell you we need to let the Holy Spirit of God prompt us in our own hearts and lives, for He indwells every believer.

God wants to lead us in the way that the psalmist described:

> *I will instruct you and teach you in the way you should go; I will guide you with My eye. Do not be like the horse*

or like the mule, which have no understanding, which must be harnessed with bit and bridle, else they will not come near you. (Psalm 32:8–9 NKJV)

What kind of a believer are you today? Do you have a bit and bridle in your mouth? A lot of Christians are like that today because that's precisely what they want: someone to pull on the bit and tell them exactly where and when to turn. But God says, "I'll guide you with My eye. I want you to stay close to Me, My Word, so you can see Me and I can lead you, prompt you, and guide you."

This always makes me think of the little girl whom I love above all others in the Old Testament—Ruth. Ruth the Moabitess came back to Bethlehem and when she got there, they were so poor she had to go out to glean.

So Ruth the Moabitess said to Naomi, "Please let me go to the field, and glean heads of grain after him in whose sight I may find favor." And she said to her, "Go, my daughter." Then she left, and went and gleaned in the field after the reapers. And she happened to come to the part of the field belonging to Boaz, who was of the family of Elimelech. (Ruth 2:2–3 NKJV)

I think this is one of the most wonderful statements in the Bible. Had you met Ruth coming out of Bethlehem that day and asked here where she was going, she would have answered, "I'm going down to glean in a field." And if you asked which field, she would have said, "I don't know." But it was very important in which field she gleaned. If she had gleaned in the wrong field, Jesus would not have been born in Bethlehem! Why not? Because if the events that are recorded in the Book of Ruth had not taken place just as they did, David would never have been born in the city of Bethlehem, and, likewise, Christ would never have been born there. But she was led to the right field—the field that fulfilled the will of God.

I'm confident that God is not a red-and-green signal light. Nor will you ever hear a voice from heaven or have the angel Gabriel appear to you. No, Ruth "happened to come" to the field that belonged to Boaz. When she got to the fields, she saw that one field had very few people working in it, which indicated to Ruth that the owner was probably a skinflint. But then she saw another field with poor people gleaning in it, so Ruth knew that the field must have belonged to a generous man.

You see, according to the Mosaic Law, widows and the poor were permitted to go into the fields of those who were harvesting grain and gather what the reapers left in the field (see Leviticus 19:9, 23:22, and Deuteronomy 24:19). Many wealthy and miserly farmers disobeyed this law, as they did all the other laws. Therefore, sometimes the poor had to search diligently before they could find a field in which they could glean. A farmer, like Boaz, who permitted the poor to glean in his fields was a keeper of the Mosaic Law, at least in that respect.

We may think it's so wonderful that Ruth made the right choice and picked the field of Boaz. But if we'd been there and told her so, I imagine she'd have said, "I know nothing about that. I prayed about it, but when I got down here and saw the two fields, I just used sanctified common sense." My friend, that's the way God leads His own.

Let me give you another illustration. The Book of Acts records the church's first council, which was held in Jerusalem. It was one of the most important councils that was ever held. In fact, the gospel of the grace of God was at stake. So we may assume that surely in that meeting the Holy Spirit would again come like wind and fire, as He had on other important occasions in church history. But He didn't. All of the leaders of the early church who were in attendance, including Peter and James, debated with the Judaizers about putting the Gentiles under the Law. When the council took their vote and decided not to put the Gentiles under the Law, they wrote:

> *For it seemed good to the Holy Spirit, and to us, to lay upon you no greater burden than these necessary things.* (Acts 15:28 NKJV)

In other words, "We prayed about it, discussed both sides of the issue, and it just seemed good to us and the Holy Spirit." These were Spirit-filled men who could be led of God, and they came to the mind of the Spirit. Oh, how we have gotten away from that today!

When the children of Israel went through the wilderness, there was a pillar of cloud and then a pillar of fire. In the Book of Numbers, we read:

So it was always: the cloud covered it by day, and the appearance of fire by night. Whenever the cloud was taken up from above the tabernacle, after that the children of Israel would journey; and in the place where the cloud settled, there the children of Israel would pitch their tents. At the command of the LORD the children of Israel would journey, and at the command of the LORD they would camp; as long as the cloud stayed above the tabernacle they remained encamped. (Numbers 9:16–18 NKJV)

If you had met Moses and Aaron in the morning and asked them, "You fellas going to travel today?" they'd have answered, "We don't know. Do you see the pillar of fire up there? It will change to a pillar of cloud in just a few moments, and if it lifts and moves out, we go. If it doesn't, we stay right here."

How many believers today are looking for the Holy Spirit of God to lead them like that? I can tell you Moses and the children of Israel never called the fire department to come put the pillar out. May I say to you that the Word of God says, "Do not quench the Spirit." Don't say no to the Spirit of God. Don't smother the Spirit. Don't get the fire extinguisher and try to put Him out by having your own way.

I can reduce this now to the lowest common denominator and make it really very simple: don't say no to the Spirit of God; say yes. Christian friend, the Word of God has you on a spot. You have to answer either yes or no—there's no middle ground. Either you quench the Spirit or you quench not the Spirit of God.

This decision is between you and the Lord, and you know in your own heart how you've answered to the Spirit of God. The Lord Jesus Christ demands total submission, or else you quench the Spirit. Some have said that living the Christian life is cheap, but where does it say that in the Word of God? It doesn't. Living the Christian life means to submit your heart and life to do anything God wants you to do, and unless you are willing to say that, you are saying no and have quenched the Spirit of God. I say that on the authority of the Word of God.

Chapter 14

THE GIFTS OF
THE SPIRIT

How wonderful it is to know that every believer has a gift from the Holy Spirit. I can't think of anything more thrilling than to know that God has given you and me a gift to function in this world, and that we are to be partners with Jesus Christ in the tremendous enterprise of making Him known!

> *But now God has set the members, each one of them, in the body just as He pleased.* (1 Corinthians 12:18 NKJV)

God is the one who sovereignly gives the gifts, and He gives them as it pleases Him. He is the one to be pleased, you see, and these gifts are in the body so that the body can function.

A man in one of my congregations had an unusual gift. He was not an usher, but he would stand in the back of the church, and if there was any kind of disruption or commotion in the service, he would take care of it. He just had a way of handling people. As I told him, he had a rare gift and one that is needed in the church. You may be surprised that something like that is a gift. Of course it is a gift, and so is cooking or sewing.

My friends, the Spirit of God is sovereign in all this. He is the one who determines what is important and what is not important. If God has called you to bake a cake or to sew a dress, then do it. That is a gift. The Holy Spirit wants us to use our gifts and to bring them under the lordship of Jesus Christ.

GIFTS UNIFY

There are diversities of gifts, but the same Spirit. There are differences of ministries, but the same Lord. And there are diversities of activities, but it is the same God who works all in all. (1 Corinthians 12:4–6 NKJV)

The Trinity is actually involved in this matter of bringing about the unity. The Holy Spirit is mentioned first: "There are diversities of gifts, but the same Spirit." The Holy Spirit distributes the gifts. "There are differences of ministries, but the same Lord"—that is the Lord Jesus Christ. The Spirit of God is the one who bestows the gifts, but the Lord Jesus Christ is the one who administers the gifts.

Then notice the work of God the Father: "And there are

diversities of activities, but it is the same God who works all in all." The word translated "activities" is in the Greek *energema*, energy. He energizes or gives power for the exercise of the gift. And God never gives a gift but that He also gives the power to exercise that gift, by the way.

So here we have something quite interesting: the *same* Spirit, the *same* Lord, and the *same* God the Father, but there are "diversities" and "differences." The purpose of the Trinity is to bring about the unity in the church, but it is unity in diversity. The Trinity is attempting to attain this unity in your church today.

Now we come to a very important verse in this matter of the unity of the Spirit:

> *But the manifestation of the Spirit is given to each one for the profit of all.* (1 Corinthians 12:7 NKJV)

We have three things here. First, the *definition of a gift*. What is a gift? Notice this: "But the manifestation of the Spirit." A gift is the manifestation of the Spirit. Therefore, if I may give you my own simple definition: a gift is the Holy Spirit using the believer to do something through him. Anything that Vernon McGee does in the flesh is useless to God, and God doesn't want it. Only what the Spirit of God does through us is of value.

This is my reason for warning many folk who have natural gifts—a natural gift of speaking, a natural gift of singing—that they should be dead sure the Holy Spirit is using that gift. Be very sure that you are not just exercising a fleshly gift, but that the Spirit of God is using you. The reason why so many church services fall flat is that we have a demonstration of a natural gift rather than the Spirit of God doing something through an individual.

Secondly, *every believer has a gift.* Notice that "the manifestation of the Spirit is given to each one." Every believer has a gift. You, if you are a child of God, have a gift. The Spirit of God has given you a gift and you are to exercise it.

Thirdly, notice the *purpose of the gift.* It is "given to each one for the profit of all." Every believer has a gift and is placed in the body of Christ to function. The gift is operational. What is the purpose? Well, the purpose is to profit the body of believers. A gift is to be used in the church to build it up, to help the church. It is never given to help you in your personal spiritual life.

For this reason, I disagree with folk who tell me (and quite a few have told me this), "Dr. McGee, we agree with you—we don't think we ought to speak in tongues in the church. We do it in our own private devotions." But, friend, that is not the purpose of a gift. It is "given to each one for the profit of all." "Profit" is the Greek *sumphero,* meaning "to bear together." No gift was ever given to be used for selfish purposes. Every gift is to be used to build up the body of believers.

Paul developed this point with an illustration of the function of members of the human body. For instance, my eye has no business running off and operating on its own. It has to operate for the benefit of the rest of the body. And that is the only way in the world a gift is to be exercised.

Different gifts are given to believers to be exercised for the good of the church; for the profit, for the wealth of, for the building up of the church—"for the profit of all."

GIFTS VARY

Then Paul made a contrast between the ordinary and the spectacular.

> *For to one is given the word of wisdom through the Spirit, to another the word of knowledge through the same Spirit, to another faith by the same Spirit, to another gifts of healings by the same Spirit, to another the working of miracles, to another prophecy, to another discerning of spirits, to another different kinds of tongues, to another the interpretation of tongues.* (1 Corinthians 12:8–10 NKJV)

He mentioned first the word of wisdom, the word of knowledge, and faith; miracles, prophecy, and tongues came later. There is a contrast here between the less exciting gifts and the more exciting gifts. In fact, back in verse 4 where he said, "There are diversities of gifts," the Greek word for "gifts" is *charisma*. Yet the charismatic movement has been confined to just one gift, tongues.

But, you see, Paul purposely made a contrast between certain gifts that are spectacular and certain gifts that are ordinary, less glamorous. The gifts of wisdom and knowledge and faith are not spectacular. Wisdom, for instance, is virtually unrecognized. Paul made a contrast by saying that it doesn't make any difference whether it is quiet wisdom or ecstatic utterances—all are needed. And he would make the comparison to the different members of the body, as we shall see.

As we move along in this chapter, notice something else concerning this matter of unity:

> *But one and the same Spirit works all these things, distributing to each one individually as He wills.* (1 Corinthians 12:11 NKJV)

Again we are told that every believer has a gift. God gives to each one a gift that is his "individually"—the Greek word is *idios*, meaning "one's own." Each one is given his own peculiar gift. Dorcas, for instance, was so valuable to the early church that Peter restored her to life (see Acts 9:36–43). You may ask, "Do you mean that a woman's ability as a seamstress is a gift from the Holy Spirit of God?" It was for Dorcas. Her gift of the Holy Spirit was that she could sew.

There are many gifts today, just as there are many members of the body—and there are hundreds of members of the body. I think one of the tragedies of the hour in the modern church is that so many believers feel as if they have no gift at all. If you are a believer, you have been put into the body of Christ and you have been placed there to function in a very definite capacity. Every believer in the church should be doing his or her own "thing." God has called you to do something.

I tell these young people who run around speaking in tongues, "Look, it's thrilling to find out what God wants *you* as a believer to do. Then do *that*. And you can do it in the power of the Holy Spirit. No one needs drugs when you can get 'high' like that. You can really get 'turned on' to that sort of thing!"

GIFTS ARE GIVEN (NOT CHOSEN)

Let me repeat verse 11:

> *But one and the same Spirit works all these things, distributing to each one individually as He wills.*

"As He wills" means that the gifts are given sovereignly by the Holy Spirit. Paul enforced this point in verse 18 of the same chapter:

> *But now God has set the members, each one of them, in the body just as He pleased.*

We do not *choose* the gifts. The Holy Spirit *gives* the gifts, and He is sovereign in this because, you see, the gifts are for the unity of the church. This matter of gifts is not a spiritual smorgasbord where you go to the table and say, "Oh, I don't want that gift of faith or that gift of wisdom. They're not romantic. I want this gift of prophecy or this gift of tongues." It's not "I want this" or "I want that." No, that's not the way it is done. Why not? Because everyone would want the same gifts. It's sort of like the barber who, while he was shaving a customer, said to him, "I'm sure glad everybody's not alike. If they were like me, they'd all want my wife." And the customer said (although he should not have), "It *is* a good thing we're not all alike, because if everybody were like me, nobody would have her!"

Fortunately, the gifts of the Spirit are not by our choice. The Spirit of God, in order to achieve unity, makes the choice for us. And I believe that in every local church, if every person were doing that which the Spirit of God wants, we would have every function that is necessary for the ongoing of the church. I think we have too many people wanting to do the same thing—when they have no gift for it. They want to do something that is showy, something that is spectacular, something that has *charisma* to it. This is the reason why speaking in tongues is so popular.

Isn't it interesting that nobody goes into orbit on these other gifts of wisdom, faith, or helps? Always, it's on tongues. You see, tongues has a certain charisma about it, and they like that type of thing. But the Holy Spirit is sovereign in this matter; He divides the gifts to us *as He wills.*

Gifts Illustrated by Members of the Body

Then Paul illustrated these gifts by a comparison to the human body.

> *For as the body is one and has many members, but all*
> *the members of that one body, being many, are one*
> *body, so also is Christ.* (1 Corinthians 12:12 NKJV)

Many members. For what purpose? One body. Although there are many members, you'll come up with only one body. And that is the way the church is to function. Many members; one body.

How do we get into the body of believers? This is very important to see and is the reason, I believe, that Dr. Luke, when he recorded the happenings on the Day of Pentecost, dared not mention the fact that they were "baptized" with the Holy Spirit. I think they were baptized, but the record says they were *filled*. Why? Because there was a service they performed: they all exercised a gift, speaking in different languages (and there was not an *unknown* tongue there that day; all were understood), and it was the filling of the Spirit that equipped them for that service.

Baptism does what? Notice especially the "one . . . all" in this verse:

> *For by one Spirit we were all baptized into one body.*
> (1 Corinthians 12:13 NKJV)

What does the Holy Spirit do? The Spirit of God, the moment you trust the Lord Jesus Christ as your Savior, regenerates you. We hear that emphasized a great deal. But He also *indwells* the believer, *seals* the believer, and *baptizes* the believer—whether the believer knows it or not. Not one of these three is an experience. But the important thing is that the Spirit of God baptizes you into the body, which means He identifies you into the body.

> *Therefore we were buried with Him through baptism* [identification] *into* [His] *death, that just as Christ was raised from the dead by the glory* [power] *of the Father, even so we also should walk in newness of life.* (Romans 6:4 NKJV)

We are identified with Christ in His death. He died *for* us, but we died *in* Him. If this were not true, then the ordinance of water baptism would have no meaning.

This is one of the reasons I'm convinced that immersion is the proper mode for water baptism, because the believer has been buried with Christ and raised with Christ. And I think that water baptism best sets forth the Spirit baptism. When Christ died all those years ago, not only did *He* die, but *I* died. I died to sin in the person of Jesus Christ when He died for me on a cross outside the walls of Jerusalem. This is the reason I will not come up for judgment. I've already been judged—Christ's judgment on the cross was my judgment. But I have been raised with Him, and I'm joined to a living Christ. Christ is the Head of the body of believers.

But He doesn't put you into the body as only a button on a garment. He puts you in the body as a member to function in the body. This is very important to see. Therefore, as I've said, this matter of getting gifts is not a spiritual smorgasbord. I'm afraid it is treated that way in our churches. Do you need a teacher for a Sunday school class? Well, pray that God will send in the teacher whom the Spirit of God wants to teach that class.

When I was a teenager, a preacher did a very foolish thing. It almost caused me to leave the church. He said to me, a sixteen-year-old boy, "Vernon, you lead the song service." I got up there—and that's when I found out I did not have the gift of music. I want to tell you, friends, it's dangerous in the Lord's work to try to do something that the Spirit of God does not want you to do.

In the following verses, Paul used some ridiculous illustrations to show that in the body there must be many members, and they all must function in order to have unity—one body.

> For in fact the body is not one member but many. If the foot should say, "Because I am not a hand, I am not of the body," is it therefore not of the body? (1 Corinthians 12:14–15 NKJV)

The foot is very important, although it is way down there on the floor covered with a shoe. A doctor in Atlanta, Georgia, once asked me, "When you are delivering a message, do you know what is the most important part of your body?" I said, "Well, I suppose it's my tongue." He said, "No, it's not. The most important part of your body is your big toe. You couldn't stand up there if it were not for your big toe."

Now suppose my big toe should say, "Look, I've been going with you for years, and when you get up there and talk, people see you but they never see me, and the two of us down here are carrying the load." Well, the folk I talk to wouldn't care about seeing my big toe. It's not pretty. But it is important. We sometimes don't appreciate the different members of our body.

Too many people misunderstand what the important gifts in the church are today. Many a preacher knows that in his congregation there are certain members who are keeping that church going. You won't see them on the platform or read their names in the bulletin, but they are the feet that are carrying it along.

Now notice Paul's next illustration:

> *And if the ear should say, "Because I am not an eye, I am not of the body," is it therefore not of the body?* (1 Corinthians 12:16 NKJV)

Suppose my ear should say, "Look, I'd like to get around there in front. People see your eyes, but they don't see your ears." Now the eyes are very important, but the body can't be all eye. If my body were all eye, I'd be just a great big overgrown basketball. The eye is a wonderful thing. It is a 3-D camera; it takes pictures and develops them instantly. There is nothing quite like the eye—but the body can't be all eye, my friend. There must be other members of the body, and this is what Paul was saying here:

> *If the whole body were an eye, where would be the hearing? If the whole were hearing, where would be the*

smelling? But now God has set the members, each one of them, in the body just as He pleased. (1 Corinthians 12:17–18 NKJV)

Then he made this personal:

Now you are the body of Christ, and members individually. (1 Corinthians 12:27 NKJV)

This is something that every one of us should remember. I'm in the body of Christ, but I'm a member individually. I am to do my "own thing" in the body of believers.

COVET THE BEST GIFTS

Paul concluded this chapter with an arresting statement:

But earnestly desire the best gifts. And yet I show you a more excellent way. (1 Corinthians 12:31 NKJV)

We'll find the "more excellent way" in 1 Corinthians 13, but notice he said to "earnestly desire the best gifts." "Desire" can mean something good, although it generally means something evil. The point here is that the Corinthians wanted the showy gifts, those which they considered to be best; therefore, Paul rebuked them, "You're desiring the showy gifts, and those are not the gifts you should be coveting. Desire the greater gifts!"

Which are the greater gifts? They are not those that make the most show, that are dramatic and exciting, but rather those that do the most good. We are to desire that which will do the most good for the body of believers. What can I do to help the church? This, my friend, is the approach that should be made, because I do believe a Christian can desire the best gifts.

THE GIFTS AND LOVE

What is this excellent way spoken of in 1 Corinthians 12:31? Well, this excellent way is the fruit of the Spirit. Now, we've already examined the fruit of the Spirit and learned that actually there is only one fruit: love. From it come all the others—joy, peace, longsuffering, kindness, goodness, faithfulness, gentleness, self-control. That wonderful bunch of delicious fruit is produced by the Holy Spirit in the life of the believer; none of these qualities can you and I produce by human effort.

The interesting thing to note here is that a gift without love is nothing, regardless of what the gift is.

> *Though I speak with the tongues of men and of angels, but have not love, I have become sounding brass or a clanging cymbal.* (1 Corinthians 13:1 NKJV)

I might have the gift of tongues in such a way that I could speak like the angel Gabriel, but without love, I am just a little jangling bell. The gift of speaking is to be exercised in love. This is something the "tongues folk" ought to consider very carefully. I don't care if you talk in tongues, but *how* do you talk in tongues? Are you doing it in love? If your gift of speaking is without love, it has no more value than the sound of a gong or a tinkling bell. For this reason we ought to be careful what we say.

Paul went on to mention other gifts:

> *And though I have the gift of prophecy, and understand all mysteries and all knowledge, and though I have all faith, so that I could remove mountains, but have not love, I am nothing.* (1 Corinthians 13:2 NKJV)

I believe prophecy here means "to preach," and I consider it to be one of the glamour gifts, by the way. "Understand all mysteries and all knowledge" are the gifts of wisdom and knowledge.

Then we come to this: "And though I have all faith"— faith is a wonderful gift. I'm part Scot and part German, and I am told that it is impossible to get more pessimism inside one skin than comes with these two nationalities. I'm a natural-born pessimist. But the Lord has always been good to me in every church I have served by putting in my congregations folk who have the gift of faith. A problem would arise in the church—my, it all looked black to me—but some brother would come up, put his arm around me, and say, "Pastor, don't you worry about this. The Lord has already shown me that this thing is going to work out." And it always did. It's a marvelous, wonderful gift. Though it's a wonderful gift, it's not a glamour gift, like speaking in tongues. It's a very quiet gift, and folk who have it are largely unknown.

Not only did Paul mention faith, but it's "faith, so that I could remove mountains." That, my friend, is a gift we could use in California, but I haven't seen many mountains moved out here, I can assure you. That's a gift very few are using today.

Then notice that Paul did a problem in arithmetic. By saying, "But have not love, I am nothing," he put a zero on the board. That's what any gift is—000000. Those half-dozen zeros are not any more than one zero. But once you put a number in front of them, then you have something. You see, a gift *with* love is something; without love it is nothing. No gift is worth anything, regardless of what it is, unless it's exercised in love. This is the reason why we ought to see the manifestation of love in the church today.

EXERCISE OF THE GIFTS

Like our Lord, Paul was a master teacher. As you know, the mark of a good teacher is the ability to take people from where they are and move them up to where they ought to be. I think that is the business of a preacher also, by the way. Paul began with the Corinthians where they were. He attempted to bring those baby Christians from their immature level up to where they should be.

Pursue love, and desire spiritual gifts, but especially that you may prophesy. (1 Corinthians 14:1 NKJV)

In other words, "Desire spiritualities, but the important thing is that you might prophesy."

Remember that to prophesy means to preach. In our day, preaching is being discounted. Many churches are even getting rid of preaching, so it's interesting that Paul put it first. I consider preaching and teaching the Word of God to be the all-important business of the church. Getting out the Word of God is *the* business of the church, and, my friend, if a church is not in that business, it would be better if the door were nailed shut. Giving out the gospel, the Word that reveals Jesus Christ, the Word that builds up believers, should be the big business of the church.

For he who speaks in a tongue does not speak to men but to God, for no one understands him; however, in the spirit he speaks mysteries. But he who prophesies speaks edification and exhortation and comfort to men. (1 Corinthians 14:2–3 NKJV)

This is the purpose of the Word of God today, and every gift given by the Spirit and used in the church should move toward that. God does not give the gift of preaching to everybody, but there are a hundred different ways in which you could help your preacher so that he could give more time to the Word of God. Everything should move to the one end of getting out the gospel. If the church is functioning like a body, whatever gift you've got will move toward the accomplishment of three things: to edify, to exhort, and to comfort.

A WORD ON TONGUES

He who speaks in a tongue edifies himself, but he who prophesies edifies the church. (1 Corinthians 14:4 NKJV)

Tongues were used for a very definite purpose, which we will see in a moment. But first, Paul presented three arguments showing the reasons why they should not speak in tongues in Corinth. The three arguments are these:

I wish you all spoke with tongues, but even more that you prophesied; for he who prophesies is greater than he who speaks with tongues, unless he interprets, that the church may receive edification. (1 Corinthians 14:5 NKJV)

Even if tongues were in the church, there must be an interpretation in order that there might be edifying of the church.

But now, brethren, if I come to you speaking with tongues, what shall I profit you unless I speak to you either by revelation, by knowledge, by prophesying [preaching], or by teaching? (1 Corinthians 14:6 NKJV)

Paul was using himself for an example. He was saying, "I'm an apostle, and I'm not going around speaking in tongues. I speak by revelation, knowledge, prophesying, and teaching."

Then he used an illustration:

Even things without life, whether flute or harp, when they make a sound, unless they make a distinction in the sounds, how will it be known what is piped or played? (1 Corinthians 14:7 NKJV)

It would make just as much sense for me to speak in tongues as to go to a piano and bang on it—and that's all I could do. It would help no one to hear me banging on a piano, but let an accomplished pianist sit down there, and we would have music. Just as you have to make sense with music, you also must make sense with your tongue.

Now I want you to notice how the tongues were used in the early church.

In the law it is written: "With men of other tongues and other lips I will speak to this people; and yet, for all that, they will not hear Me," says the Lord. (1 Corinthians 14:21 NKJV)

Who are "this people"? It's Israel. Here is a quotation from Isaiah, written about seven hundred years before Christ came to earth. God said, concerning His people Israel, that He had sent them prophets, He had given them the Word of God, He had chastised them, He had tried to speak to them in every way possible to bring them back to Himself, but they would not hear Him. Then He said He would give them at some future time a sign:

> *For with stammering lips and another tongue He will speak to this people, to whom He said, "This is the rest with which you may cause the weary to rest," and, "This is the refreshing"; yet they would not hear.* (Isaiah 28:11–12 NKJV)

In other words, God told them that there was a day coming when He would speak to them with other tongues—not *unknown* tongues, but *other* tongues. More than seven hundred years later, in Jerusalem on the Day of Pentecost, the apostles of our Lord spoke in many different tongues. All the people who heard them were Israelites and had come to Jerusalem from various parts of the Roman Empire. There wasn't a Gentile in the crowd that day. And these instructed Jews were reminded of Isaiah's prophecy.

A number of years later Paul was in Corinth and began his ministry at the great synagogue (as recorded in Acts 18). That is where he preached the gospel until the unbelieving Jews finally put him out. Those who believed formed a little church made up of both Jews and Gentiles, largely Gentiles. And these new believers spoke in tongues (see 1 Corinthians 14). What did it mean? It meant this: these proud unbelieving Jews were walking around saying, "That little crowd of

Gentiles over there say *they* are God's chosen people. Don't they know *we* are God's people? *We* are the chosen people. We're *it*." Then they heard that little group speak in tongues, and the instructed Israelites said, "Wait a minute. Is God giving us His final word? Is this His final message to us? He said in Isaiah that He would try every means to speak to us, and we would not hear." And some of the Jews turned to Christ. Most of them did not. But it was God's final word to the nation.

In Paul's letter to the Corinthians, he reminded them of the purpose of tongues:

> *Therefore tongues are for a sign, not to those who believe but to unbelievers; but prophesying is not for unbelievers but for those who believe.* (1 Corinthians 14:22 NKJV)

To those unbelieving Jews, it was a sign.

Now as far as I know, there is not a group in existence today using tongues as God intended them to be used. If they are using them to speak to the nation Israel, I'll buy it. Tongues were meant to be a sign to the nation Israel. That is the reason why thousands turned to Christ on the Day of Pentecost and during the days that followed. It was God sending out His last call to His people.

> *Therefore if the whole church comes together in one place, and all speak with tongues, and there come in those who are uninformed or unbelievers, will they not say that you*

are out of your mind? But if all prophesy, and an unbeliever or an uninformed person comes in, he is convinced by all, he is convicted by all. (1 Corinthians 14:23–24 NKJV)

We do not want a stranger to step into the church and think he has entered into a group of people who have gone mad. If there is one thing we need today, it is the logical, meaningful presentation of the Word of God. People in this world are intelligent, they are scientific, they are sophisticated. They want a logical message that can be understood. The Word of God needs to be presented so it can be understood.

Therefore, brethren, desire earnestly to prophesy.
(1 Corinthians 14:39 NKJV)

As I have said, prophecy is a gift we should want in order to get the Word of God out. To me, the most thrilling thing in the world is to see people who want to hear the Word of God. Oh, that God would give His church a desire to get the Word of God out today!

How can it be done? Believers in the church have gifts— gifts of administration, of giving, all kinds of gifts—that God uses to get out the Word. What is your gift? You can do something to get the Word of God out in these days.

Let's each apply this to our own lives. If you are a believer, a Christian, it is because you have trusted Christ. And when you trusted Christ, the Holy Spirit not only regenerated you, He also baptized you, which means He put you in the body of believers. Now the body is made up of many members, and He gave you and each member of the body a gift and a place to function. My question is: are you exercising your gift? Are you doing your "thing" in the church? Are you building up the body of believers? This should be the purpose and desire of every Christian today.

Chapter 15

WALKING IN
THE SPIRIT

I say then: Walk in the Spirit, and you shall not fulfill the lust of the flesh. (Galatians 5:16 NKJV)

God has given to us clear-cut commands relative to our relationship with the Holy Spirit. These are of utmost importance! To obey these commands of Christ is to experience the power, the peace, and the joy that are God's will for all of His children today.

Some folk seem to think that they need to be all pepped up or hepped up—then, *zoop!* up they go. But, my friend, you do not go into orbit living the Christian life; you walk on solid earth. The Christian life is not an occasional flight into space; it is a day-by-day walk down the streets of our cities, in our neighborhoods, in our places of business, and in our homes. *The believer is to walk in the Holy Spirit.*

The Christian life requires a discipline that is far more demanding than that which is required by any ideology, military service, or organization. I suppose the reason for all the tragic failures, frightful causalities, and total wrecks that line the shore of life is that we have not taken seriously the command: *walk in the Spirit.*

Walking in the Spirit literally means to walk by means of the Holy Spirit. It is the present tense—*continue* to walk. In other words, it is a constant, continual, habitual, unbroken, moment-by-moment walk. The walk of most of us Christians is up and down, off and on, hit and miss. But there should not be even a second when a child of God is not walking by means of the Holy Spirit.

By means of simply means that we are assigning to another that which we cannot do ourselves. Let me illustrate. Suppose you were to board the train in Los Angeles, intending to go to Chicago. When the train reaches the desert, it stops. You wait, and you wait, and you wait. Wondering what is the matter, you get off and go to the rear of the train where you find the engineer trying to push the caboose! You exclaim, "What in the world are you doing?" He tells you, "I'm trying to get this train moving." "But," you say, "your place is up front. You just pull the throttle and the train will take off." You see, that diesel engine will do what a mere man cannot do.

It is ridiculous, I know, to imagine an engineer trying to push a train, but there are a lot of Christians today who are attempting to live just that way. They are like the salesman in the South who came rushing into the station just as the train was pulling out. Thinking he still might make it, he took out at a run down the track with suitcase in hand. Every second the distance lengthened between him and the train. Finally, he gave up and turned dejectedly back to the station. One of the natives, sitting on the lone express wagon, asked as he passed, "Did you miss your train?" "No," the salesman replied, "I just love to chase them out of the station." Christian living for a great many folk is just chasing the train out of the station. We never seem to get on board.

God presents to us a new way of living. Paul expressed it as he wrote to the Galatian believers:

> *For in Christ Jesus neither circumcision nor uncircumcision avails anything, but faith working through love.* (Galatians 5:6 NKJV)

It is no longer by law, no longer by works, but by faith (a new principle) working by love. It is a new formula, a new prescription, different from anything that has been offered in the past.

In the past, God said to His people:

> *I will set My tabernacle among you, and My soul shall not abhor you. I will walk among you and be your God, and you shall be My people.* (Leviticus 26:11–12 NKJV)

Back in the Old Testament, God said to His people, "I will be *among* you. I will walk *with* you." But here is something altogether different. He says now, "I will walk *in* you." That is what it means to walk by means of the Holy Spirit.

We who have been saved by faith often wonder why the unsaved rebel against the gospel of grace. Why do they feel they have to *do* something for God in order to be saved? God says they can do nothing but accept what He has done for them. He paid the penalty for sin by giving His Son to die. Christ died, was buried, paid the penalty in full, and was raised in newness of life. Now faith in Him will save us! We marvel that the natural man rebels against accepting such a wonderful provision.

Yet how many Christians rebel against the walk of faith? That was the major problem with the Galatian Christians:

> *O foolish Galatians! Who has bewitched you that you should not obey the truth, before whose eyes Jesus Christ was clearly portrayed among you as crucified? This only I want to learn from you: Did you receive the Spirit by the works of the law, or by the hearing of faith? Are you so foolish? Having begun in the Spirit, are you now being made perfect by the flesh?* (Galatians 3:1–3 NKJV)

Paul was saying, "You have been saved by faith, the Holy Spirit has regenerated you. Now you are to continue by the same method—walk by faith in the power of the Holy Spirit."

> *You have become estranged from Christ, you who attempt to be justified by law; you have fallen from grace. For we*

through the Spirit eagerly wait for the hope of righteousness by faith. (Galatians 5:4–5 NKJV)

He was saying to them, "You were saved by *grace*—that is a high plane. Now do not drop down to a lower plane by attempting to live by the Law or some legal system. Continue to live by faith, walking in the power of the Holy Spirit."

If we can lay hold of this new truth, it will mean that a new day has dawned for us. It is a new life. We will experience a new joy, a new freedom, and a new peace. God wants us to live where there is the greatest fulfillment of life. He has the best for us, and He wants us to have His best—not His second best, or His third.

This great subject does not rest on a few isolated texts, or on some "proof texts" and unrelated Scripture. It is the great theme of the Word of God. God wants His child to walk in the way that will bring the greatest amount of satisfaction and service.

Now there are three steps that must be taken in order to walk by means of the Spirit.

STEP ONE—REALIZE

In walking, you always have to take a first step. The first step in walking by the Spirit is a realization of our human weakness and sin. Because it seems like a strange beginning, many believers will not start there. But notice where God begins:

> *If we say that we have no sin, we deceive ourselves, and the truth is not in us.* (1 John 1:8 NKJV)

This is the most difficult step of all; always, the first step is most difficult. It is like the first step of a baby who stands there rocking, wondering whether he dare try, afraid he might fall. He is moving out into something that is entirely new, and he hesitates.

For many believers, this first step is new, and we are unwilling to take the place of utter helplessness, total corruption, and absolute depravity before God. Many believers refuse this first step, saying, "I am just as good as the next fellow. I don't do this and I don't do that." My beloved, self-satisfaction never leads you to a walk by the Spirit.

> *If we say that we have fellowship with Him, and walk in darkness, we lie and do not practice the truth. But if we walk in the light as He is in the light, we have fellowship with one another, and the blood of Jesus Christ His Son cleanses us from all sin. If we say that we have no sin, we deceive ourselves, and the truth is not in us.* (1 John 1:6–8 NKJV)

Actually, we are not now talking about sins, but about the sin nature. When you and I came to Christ and trusted Him, we were given a new nature. Yet that old nature abides with us. It is even more alert after conversion. The old nature that you and I have is a terrible thing, and frightful terms are used to describe it. John spoke of the "*lust* of the flesh" (Galatians 5:16 NKJV, emphasis mine)—that is the old nature. It is as a running sore filled with pus and corruption. Someone has said that if we could see ourselves as God sees us, we could not tolerate ourselves.

The old nature is a body of death, a putrefying corpse that we are carrying around. We cannot even embalm it, and it smells to high heaven! Now don't you say that you do not have an old nature. Don't sit there and look pious, as though all of this were far removed from where you live. My friend, every child of God has this old nature, and the greatest saints have been more conscious of it than anyone else.

David, with a broken heart, prayed, "Behold, I was brought forth in iniquity, and in sin my mother conceived me" (Psalm 51:5 NKJV). Isaiah, keenly conscious of his sin in the presence of God's holiness, cried, "Woe is me, for I am undone! Because I am a man of unclean lips, and I dwell in the midst of a people of unclean lips; for my eyes have seen the King, the LORD of hosts" (Isaiah 6:5 NKJV). Jeremiah, the weeping prophet, declared, "The heart is deceitful above all things, and desperately wicked; who can know it?" (Jeremiah 17:9 NKJV). Even the great apostle Paul had a sin nature: "O wretched man that I am! Who will deliver me from this body of death?" (Romans 7:24 NKJV).

When the child of God comes to the place where he cries in agony, "Who shall deliver me from this old nature that is dragging me down? I want to be free from the pull of a fallen nature," he has taken the first step toward walking by the Holy Spirit. Step one is a realization of our sin nature and our human weakness.

STEP TWO—RECOGNIZE

Now for the second step. There must be a recognition that God's standard for Christian living is not attainable by human effort or ability. Notice again these words:

> *You have become estranged from Christ, you who attempt to be justified by law; you have fallen from grace.*
> (Galatians 5:4 NKJV)

The reason that we are not under the Mosaic Law today—not under even part of it—is that God has called us to a higher plane than the Law. God has set before us a standard that is infinitely higher and, humanly speaking, unattainable. God has already said that you and I *cannot* live the Christian life. It is impossible.

Now notice the standard God sets for His children today:

> *But you are a chosen generation, a royal priesthood, a holy nation, His own special people, that you may proclaim the praises of Him who called you out of darkness into His marvelous light.* (1 Peter 2:9 NKJV)

A standard of showing forth the praises of God! There are those who say that since we have been saved by grace, we can do as we please. Such is not the case. There are commandments for the Christian. No child of God can do as he pleases; he must do as *Christ* pleases. The reason we are not under the Ten Commandments is that we have graduated to a higher level. Christ said,

> *A new commandment I give to you, that you love one another; as I have loved you, that you also love one another.* (John 13:34 NKJV)

Be honest now. Are you able to love another believer as Christ loves him? If you are truthful, you will have to say, "I fall short." God puts before us an impossible standard—yet these are Christ's commandments.

He also said,

> *If you love Me, keep My commandments . . . If you keep My commandments, you will abide in My love, just as I have kept My Father's commandments and abide in His love. These things I have spoken to you, that My joy may remain in you, and that your joy may be full. This is My commandment, that you love one another as I have loved you.* (John 14:15; 15:10–12 NKJV)

This is a standard so high that we must fall down before God and confess that we cannot measure up to it in our own strength.

But this is not all. There are other commandments.

> *Finally then, brethren, we urge and exhort in the Lord Jesus that you should abound more and more, just as you received from us how you ought to walk and to please*

God; for you know what commandments we gave you through the Lord Jesus. (1 Thessalonians 4:1–2 NKJV)

Then, turning to the last chapter of this epistle, we find that Paul gave not ten commandments, but twenty-two! Here are a few:

Rejoice always. (1 Thessalonians 5:16 NKJV)

When you awake to a morning flooded with sunshine and the song of birds, and everything is coming your way, of course you rejoice! But what about that dark day, when your world has tumbled about you, when you were even betrayed by friends? Did you rejoice?

Pray without ceasing. (1 Thessalonians 5:17 NKJV)

We are to maintain an attitude of prayer, which means that our prayer does not end when we say "Amen." We are to move out in a workaday world in communion with God. Do you do that?

In everything give thanks; for this is the will of God in Christ Jesus for you. (1 Thessalonians 5:18 NKJV)

How are you doing with that commandment? Do you give thanks for everything?

Paul, writing to the Corinthian Christians, said:

Casting down arguments and every high thing that exalts itself against the knowledge of God, bringing every thought into captivity to the obedience of Christ. (2 Corinthians 10:5 NKJV)

Is every thought that enters your mind brought to the obedience of Christ? When that fellow cut in ahead of you on the freeway this morning, was that thought brought to the obedience of Christ? Oh, my friend, there are commandments that any honest person looks at and cries out, "I can't do it, I fall short!" God's standard is unattainable by human effort.

This realization is the second step in walking by means of the Holy Spirit. God wants us to know that we have this old nature that is in rebellion against Him—it never does anything right. When you take these two steps: (1) realizing your human weakness and sin, and (2) recognizing that God's standard is unattainable by your own effort, then God is ready to meet you. This brings us to the third step.

STEP THREE—REST

The third and last step is to *rest* on the Holy Spirit—depend on Him to do for us that which we cannot do. This brings us back to our text.

I say then: Walk in the Spirit, and you shall not fulfill the lust of the flesh. (Galatians 5:16 NKJV)

Now consider with me this matter of walking. We talk without thinking. We can go down the street thinking about something else while we are walking. But, you know, we had a great problem getting started. Remember that little fellow trying to take his first wobbly step and toppling over. If we stop walking for one second, it is no longer walking—it is standing. You have to keep going. You put one foot in front, then you have to bring up the other foot, and then you have to do it all over again. It is a moment-by-moment, continual, habitual thing.

It is interesting how the Word of God has brought together metaphors. The Christian life is a conflict, and in the conflict we are told to *stand*—"Stand therefore," Paul said to the Ephesians (6:14 NKJV). Also, the Christian life is a race, and we are told to "*Run . . . the race*" (Hebrews 12:1 NKJV). But the greater part of the Christian life is just plain living, and that means *walking*—which is the most difficult.

Many of us can move out onto the arena of life, and when there comes the applause from the gallery we can draw our sword and stand our ground. Or when those on the sidelines are urging us to run, we can exert great effort. But when we get up in the morning to a sink full of dirty dishes, or go down to the office to a desk loaded with accumulated work, we fail. It is then that we are to *walk* by the power of the Holy Spirit.

And we are to walk by faith and not by sight. Let us come back to Galatians 5:5 (NKJV), "For we through the Spirit eagerly wait for the hope of righteousness by faith." The whole Christian life, from the moment we are born again until we come into His presence, is a walk by faith—a faith that rests upon the indwelling Holy Spirit.

Let me use a homely illustration. I used to see a little old lady who moved about with the aid of a walker, a little enclosure on wheels. She would come down the sidewalk, only a short distance at a time, and then she would stop and rest. As I watched her, I would think of the Christian life being something like that. I long to get to the place to which she had come. My problem is that I say, "Oh, have done with this little cage I'm in. I'm strong enough to walk by myself." I do not take one step until I am on my face.

Has that been your experience? We imagine we have the power and strength in and of ourselves to walk; we do not. We have to walk by the Holy Spirit. We must be utterly dependent upon and constantly resting upon the Holy Spirit, somewhat as that little old lady depended upon her walker.

My friend, you and I live in a difficult day. The devil is out to deceive and sidetrack us. We need to stay close to the Word of God. The entire bent of our lives should be to know Christ and to please Him. He reveals Himself and reveals His will for us through His Word, so study the Word. See what He cautions against and what He commands. Appropriate the provisions He has made for our walk down here.

We need to start each day with God, *realizing* our human weakness and the presence of our old nature, *recognizing* and confessing to Him our inability to meet His standard, and *resting* by faith in the power of the indwelling Holy Spirit to accomplish what we cannot do.

Beloved, if we live in the Spirit, let us also walk in the Spirit—for Jesus' sake.